Shattered Lives

Portraits From America's Drug War

By Mikki Norris, Chris Conrad & Virginia Resner

Creative Xpressions PO Box 1716, El Cerrito, California 94530 USA
ISBN 0-9639754-4-7 ©1998. First Printing 1998. All rights reserved.

Copyright © 1998 by Mikki Norris, Chris Conrad & Virginia Resner.

Shattered Lives: Portraits From America's Drug War
(Based on the Human Rights and the Drug War Exhibit)

By Mikki Norris, Chris Conrad & Virginia Resner

ISBN 0-9639754-4-7. First edition. First Printing, 1998.
Creative Xpressions, El Cerrito, California USA

Library of Congress Cataloging Data
Norris, Monica; Conrad, Chris; and Resner, Virginia
Shattered Lives: Portraits from America's Drug War /
    Norris, Conrad and Resner
    Includes index
    ISBN 0-9639754-4-7

Acknowledgements
The authors and publisher wish to thank the following persons and organizations: Agape Foundation, Michelle Aldrich, Dan Baum, Dr. John Beresford, Kathy Bergman, Melina Bloomfield, Sandee Burbank, Business Alliance for Commerce in Hemp, Cannabis Action Network, Center on Juvenile and Criminal Justice, Common Sense for Drug Policy, Ed Denson, Rick Doblin, Amy Doktor, Leslie Donovan, DRC Net, Drug Policy Forum of Texas, Drug Policy Foundation, Drug War prisoners, Don Duncan, Richard Dwyer, Richard Evans, Families Against Mandatory Minimums, Family Council on Drug Awareness, Robert Field, George, Everett Gholston, Dale Gieringer, Peter Gorman, Brenda Grantland, Mark Greer, High Hopes Foundation, Jodie Israel, Heather Jordan, Justice Policy Institute, JusticeWorks Community, Alysson Kohn, Ellen Komp, Mario Lap, Julie Larson, Richard Lee, Lindesmith Center, Lorri, Bernice and Clarence Malin, Marijuana Policy Project, Mark Mauer, Rosie Misenhimer, Multidisciplinary Association for Psychedelic Studies, Ethan Nadelmann, Louis G. Norris, November Coalition, Wm. G. Panzer, Caroljo Papac, Amy Pofahl, Monica Pratt, Herb Resner, Hillel Resner, Marsha Rosenbaum, Jim Rosenfield, the Sentencing Project, Amy Shutkin, Eric Sterling, Julie Stewart, Jeffrey Stonehill, Kirk Warren, Mark Weiman, Connie Williams, Don Wirtshafter, Richard B. Wolf, Kendra Wright, Kevin Zeese, all those who have provided encouragement for this production, and many others who contributed in so many important ways.

Special Acknowledgements and credits
Scott Braley, for needle exchange photos
Bill Bridges, for Frances Plante photo
Civil Liberties Monitoring Project, for CAMP photos
John Donovan, for graphic assistance
James Evans, for Esequiel Hernandez photos
Carol Hyams, for photo of authors on the back cover
Peter King and Lissie Fein, for the cover design
R.U. Sirius, for editorial assistance

Printed and bound in the USA by Gilliland Printing.
Typeset in Palatino, Helvetica, and Courier fonts.
Cover fonts: Impact and Euro.

For use questions, contact Creative Xpressions.
PO Box 1716, El Cerrito, California 94530 USA
510-215-8326. www.hr95.org.

On the cover:
Amy Pofahl, Danielle Metz family, William Foster family.
See index for page numbers of their stories.

Key to photos on page iii, from left to right, top to bottom:
Numbered pages are black and white, lettered pages are in full color and inserted after page 70.

Kevin Alexander, page C.
Ernie Montgomery, page J.
Lexi Bauer, page L.
Corey Stringfellow, page B.

Vivienne Hopkins, page 45.
Shirley Womble, page E.
Corey Woodfolk, age 29, serving 50 years, charged with conspiracy to distribute 1 kilo of heroin.
Laichem SaeLee page 46, 47, J

Melinda George, page 22.
Greg Kinder, page 34.
Mark Printz, page 35, H.
Valerie Johnson, page 20, E.

Alfreda Robinson, page 39, F.
Debi Campbell, age 43, serving 19 years 6 months, charged with conspiracy to distribute methamphetamine.
Lewis 'Skip' Atley, page 79.
Kay Tanner, page 11, G.

Contents

*This book is dedicated
to the prisoners and victims of the Drug War;
to their families and friends; and
to all who advocate for a just and
peaceful end to the Drug War
with full recognition of Human Rights, and
liberty and justice for all.*

Special Dedication

In loving memory of

Steven Faulkner

1949–1998

Former Drug War POW and
Virginia Resner's long-time companion.

His arrest and imprisonment helped inspire this work;
his words and support for human rights helped
    carry the message of justice;
his untimely death soon after his release has been a
    great loss to us all.
We honor and miss him.

The Human Rights and the Drug War exhibit has been seen throughout the US, and parts of Canada and Europe. California showings included the Oakland City Hall, the San Francisco Main Library (above), and Stanford University (left).

Human Rights and the Drug War

"Make injustice visible." — Mahatma Ghandi.

Shattered Lives is based on an exhibit project entitled, Human Rights and the Drug War. It began in 1995, in conjunction with the United Nations' 50th anniversary, when we recognized a unique opportunity to display the "human face of the Drug War" to the world community visiting San Francisco for UN activities. Human Rights and the Drug War is a collaborative project that views the Drug War in the context of its violations of the UN Universal Declaration of Human Rights and the American Bill of Rights. Since the United States presents itself as a global policeman on human rights and is quick to point its finger at other countries for their violations, we felt it was time for America to take a look at itself.

It came together when Mikki Norris and Chris Conrad of the Family Council on Drug Awareness met Virginia Resner, California representative for Families Against Mandatory Minimums. We quickly formed a coalition with the added support of Forfeiture Endangers Americans Rights and about a dozen other groups and individuals. We called it Human Rights 95, or HR 95 for short.

The first showing was unveiled as *Atrocities of the Drug War* at Fort Mason, in San Francisco on June 24, 1995. At the same time we held an event entitled "Give Drug Peace a Chance" at which we proposed a Drug War Truce.

Over the past three years, we have taken the exhibit to community centers, libraries, churches, universities, public buildings, conferences, and festivals throughout the United States. We designed a display for the Drugs Peace House in Amsterdam, The Netherlands, which went on to Heidelberg, Germany and later to London, England. In 1996, we were proud to receive an award from the Committee on Unjust Sentencing for "Valorous conduct in the War on Drugs," accompanied by a certificate that was made by hand by women inmates from FPC Dublin.

Since its inception, we have designed many different versions of the displays, such as, Prisoners of the Drug War, Uncle Sam's Warehouse, and Human Rights and the Drug War. To meet the great demand for the exhibit, we now create thematic displays for other groups to bring awareness to the general public and policy makers about the human casualties and costs of the US Drug War.

— *The authors*

**Jodie Israel and Calvin Treiber's children in Montana. Tracy holds Calvin Jr.,
Laura is in front.**

*"They have made orphans of the children.
They cry and miss their parents, who they love
and were good to them."*

—Winnie Crowley, mother of Jodie Israel

Preface

Coming face to face with the victims of America's Drug War

I was a child in the 1950s, a decade after the Second World War and the Nazi Holocaust.

I remember the conversations I had with my father and mother about the injustice that a government can inflict upon its people. I was taught that it was wrong to scapegoat a group of people, to blame them for society's ills, and to treat people with such inhumanity. We learned that we must always remember that scapegoating and genocide are wrong, and we must never let it happen again.

In the Eighties, I met a German who told me that his parents said that they didn't know what was going on during the War. That was their excuse for going along with the Nazi government. This young man, who was politically active in many struggles for social justice, said that he had to be involved and do something, because he could not use the excuse his parents had given. His knowledge compelled him to action, citing the old adage, 'If you're not part of the solution, you're part of the problem'.

In 1995, someone handed me photos of a young woman and her children, including the photo on the facing page, which were accompanied by a fax from her mother. It said, "Can you help us? They have made orphans of the children." The mother then explained that the government had just sentenced her daughter, Jodie Israel, to eleven years and her son-in-law, Calvin Treiber, to 26 years for a first-time, non-violent drug offense. Though there was little evidence to implicate her daughter, she was rounded up with other members of the community in a marijuana conspiracy case.

Looking at the photo of her innocent, young children, I was struck by the injustice of destroying these children's lives. What did these young people do to deserve this punishment? Why should they be forced to grow up without their parents?

It triggered memories of emotions I had when I lost my own father at age thirteen. The loss of his support, his love, his being there for me was devastating. Life seemed so unfair.

Jodie and Calvin's children must be feeling the same way. And what did the parents do to deserve to be locked away for so long, to miss the raising of their own children, to waste away their own lives? Non-violent consensual offenses. Why were these first-time, non-violent offenders being punished more severely than violent offenders who kill or rape or molest others? Who gains from it? Who does it hurt?

I have read the stories of these and other non-violent drug offenders and visions of the Holocaust haunt me again. I see how America's prisons are turning into concentration camps for the drug culture. About sixty percent of federal prisoners are now incarcerated for drug offenses. The US government has demonized and declared war against a certain group of people. In the name of the Drug War, it is now okay to violate them; to take their homes and property, to shatter their lives and destroy families, to incarcerate their loved ones for long periods of time, to strip them of their rights.

What kind of future lies ahead for America and its people? Where does this path lead?

In *Shattered Lives: Portraits from America's Drug War*, you will find out what's really going on in America today. You will lose your excuse for allowing your tax dollars to go toward perpetuating this inhumanity.

This was the lesson of the Holocaust: "Never again." We must recognize the insidious nature of the Drug War and put an end to its injustice, before it is too late; before *you* or someone you love is the next one caught in the ever broadening net of this merciless Drug War.

— *Mikki Norris*

About these photos and stories

The photos and stories you are about to see were mostly sent to us by the prisoners themselves, or their families or friends.

Locked away and forgotten, many Prisoners of the Drug War (POWs) feel that this project is their only link to the outside world, their only chance for their plights to be communicated, and their only hope for a change in their situation. We believe they have a right to be heard, and have taken upon ourselves this task of bringing them to you.

Many of the photos used in this book were taken by inmate photographers on visiting day. Some include friends and family members who were not identified to us.

The sentences and charges conveyed here reflect the information we had at the time of printing. Some POWs are several years into their sentences already; some are near the end and on their way to half-way houses. Some have just started serving time. Many POWs have been working on appeals through the court systems, searching for relief from the portion of their lives that they will have to spend behind bars. There will hopefully be some changes. In the interests of justice, we wish them luck and success in their appeals, and a second chance at life on the outside.

The information in this book is like a snapshot of America and the Drug War as they were when we went to press. We have made every reasonable effort to be accurate in this depiction. Statistics are constantly shifting, and are drawn from public sources including government reports and a variety of research groups. We hope you benefit from this information.

I.
The Big Picture

Donald Scott didn't smoke marijuana, but in the end that didn't matter. The end came for Donald in his California home early one October morning, in a deadly hail of bullets fired by a group of armed men. They planned to take his property, according to an investigation and report by Ventura County District Attorney Michael Bradbury.

The county coroner summarized the events of that bloody morning in a single word: "homicide." Police know exactly who the gunmen were, who hired them, and where they work. Yet, no one has ever been charged with this crime.

How did they get away with murder? The Drug War. Scott was shot as part of a police action by a multi-jurisdictional drug task force: a paramilitary operation by government agencies. Taxpayers bought the bullets that ripped apart his chest and head and left him bleeding on his floor. No one was fired or reprimanded for his death.

No one even bothered to apologize.

Anything can be rationalized in the name of the Drug War. Human life is just expendable collateral damage. Constitutional rights are ignored — a minor inconvenience. Generations of Americans are sacrificed to feed the insatiable appetite of a growing prison industrial complex. Prison labor has become a profitable sideline for a variety of corporate interests, as has building prisons, and guarding and feeding inmates. No expense is too big to pass on to the taxpayers. No lie is too big to tell. No freedom is too precious to discard.

For a significant number of its citizens, America has become a land of police spies, prosecutorial courts, and lifetimes spent behind bars over nonviolent offenses. The politicians say they're sending a message to kids, but drug use continues to rise and fall on its own, regardless of the war. Drugs remain readily available on the streets and in the schools. Add to that the mass marketing of tobacco, alcohol and pharmaceutical drugs, plus the denial of adequate medication for patients in chronic pain, and you get a sense of how out-of-control our drug control policy has become. In the ultimate expression of Drug War failure, illegal drugs are sold in the prisons, often by the guards.

Why does a nation choose to abandon its schools and squander its wealth on a policy with no visible benefit? It's not about drugs. It's about money: prison contracts, property seizure, and criminal market profits. It's about power. The power to control how people live, what they think, with whom they associate; power to destroy lives over merest suspicion or rumor. Power to control society to submit to any political wind.

Well-paid bureaucrats scrutinize the legal system for glimmers of compassion, discretion and freedom, to seal off these 'loopholes.' Drug warriors write Anti-This Acts and Omnibus-That Laws and stifle political dissent. Human rights violations and conflicts of interest within the prison and law enforcement industries are accepted as consequences of waging war.

If you think you are somehow safe because you don't use drugs or you only smoke a little medical marijuana now and then as needed, you are terribly, tragically wrong.

Donald Scott was shot in his own home by drug police acting on false information.

Portraits from the Drug War

Donald Scott didn't use illegal drugs. He was a millionaire who had a valuable parcel of land that government agencies hoped to confiscate after they raided his home. Under forfeiture law, a verdict of not guilty of drug charges still allows the government to seize their victim's private property.

Donald became just one of the uncounted casualties of the Drug War. He died in 1992 without ever knowing who the armed men were that kicked in his front door, or why they were there. His story is one of many you will encounter in this book.

Be forewarned, these stories may shock and upset you. But you need to be aware of what is happening in America today, because what you *don't* know can hurt you — and those you love — very, very badly.

Addicted to the Drug War

The monotonous, dehumanizing routine of the Drug War grinds on. News media play on public fears to sell copy. Another record size property seizure; more mothers in prison; one marijuana arrest every 49 seconds — over eleven million cannabis busts so far; the biggest law enforcement budgets in history, the most sweeping and intrusive police powers ever, gangs and corruption! Politicians push their 'tough on crime' image. Every year, they ban more activities and pass longer prison sentences, more forfeiture laws, and higher enforcement budgets. The next year, they mindlessly repeat this compulsive habit.

Our government shows advanced symptoms of Drug War addiction. Politicians habitually increase their drug law dosage. Constantly looking for a stronger fix, they spend the nation into debt without getting satisfaction. Our leaders refuse to admit the destructive consequences of their behavior. Drug enforcement agents abuse the public trust and resort to brutality and lies. News media reinforce the negative behavior of both police and drug users. Like a co-dependent partner, they live in morbid denial of their own role. Paid informants prosper from setting up other people for arrest and prosecution. Drugs, disease, violence and rape are common within the prisons, and the future is ominous, indeed.

An American nightmare

In the past thirty years, the United States has gone from being 'The Land of the Free' to one of the world's biggest prison states. America incarcerates more of its citizens than any other developed nation except Russia. Almost two-thirds of federal prisoners are charged with drug activities that were not even illegal at the beginning of this century.

The Drug War's hysteria, propaganda and scapegoating have frightening parallels to Nazi Germany. This forces us to ask if we are now in the early stages of a more subtle form of social genocide, with prisons in place of concentration camps. It makes an easy to whip-up recipe for an American nightmare.

Take a political agenda with a biased, simplistic media campaign. Sprinkle in government agencies and private media groups to blame all the ills of society on a 'drug culture'. Scapegoat a disempowered minority, and set it aside. To the mix, add expanded police powers, no-knock searches, random and mandatory drug tests, secret police and instigators, and laws that disproportionately punish drug offenders. Shake well and cover up.

Now, go get your minority group. Brand them 'criminals' or 'addicts' and baste with the politically-correct term 'zero tolerance.' Dehumanize them by referring only to 'drugs' and never to 'consenting adults.' Turn up the heat by seizing their homes, bank accounts, valuables, and businesses.

Cook them thoroughly by taking their rights and privileges, like drivers licenses, social and educational benefits, jobs and housing. Punish loyalty and encourage families, neighbors and friends to betray each other for personal gain or for survival. Sear with ever more savage penalties on those who defy the state. Institute mass incarcerations, drain off the target community from society and concentrate them by the thousands into prison and work camps. Season to taste, and watch for signs of smoke.

As a nation we have very nearly cooked our own goose, and there is no time to spare. In its zeal to eradicate marijuana, Congress passed a 1994 crime bill that would have sentenced to death our Founding Fathers for growing fiber hemp. Murderers and rapists are let out of prison earlier than nonviolent drug offenders.

With House Speaker Newt Gingrich advocating the death penalty for anyone caught with more than 100 doses of any illegal drug (less than a quarter pound of marijuana), and a Texas official calling to speed up executions by replacing the electric chair with an "electric couch", are we nearing the final solution to drugs?

Lost in the frenzy is this simple fact. Illicit drug offenders are people, too. They retain all their human rights. Most casual drug users are peaceful, productive members of society until they become casualties of the Drug War.

It is not too late to change the recipe of our drug policy from war to tolerance, compassion, dignity and respect for human rights. It's time to wake up to what is going on around us. These are our neighbors, our friends; our families who are being destroyed.

Masked and heavily armed, national guard troops patrol northern California in Operation Green Sweep, to search and destroy marijuana gardens and round up suspects. This group turned up the driveway to the wrong home.
Photo: Civil Liberties Monitoring Project.

Reviving our human rights

In the wake of the Nazi Holocaust, to prevent its recurrence, the member states of the United Nations adopted the UN Universal Declaration of Human Rights.

Its Preamble states that "The General Assembly proclaims this Universal Declaration of Human Rights as a common standard of achievement for all peoples and all nations, to the end that every individual and every organ of society, keeping this Declaration constantly in mind, shall strive by teaching and education to promote respect for these rights and freedoms and by progressive measures, national and international, to secure their universal and effective recognition and observance."

That is what this book is about. It's not about drugs. It's about human lives and rights. It's about families and their personal stories. It's about how far astray America has gone, and it's about how to get back on track before it's too late. Fortunately there is still time for a second chance, both for the victims of the Drug War and for society itself. This book seeks to move that process forward.

After all, we're in this together.

— *Chris Conrad*

In the Heartland of America

In the heartland of America
a war is underway
directed at our families
it worsens day by day.

It's not led by foreign entities
as it rips across our land
for the leader of this travesty
is our good old Uncle Sam.

In the name of law and order
his men invade our homes
They take, destroy and rampage,
read our mail and tap our phones;

They confiscate our properties,
lock away our citizens in jail,
steal the money from our bank accounts
and then deny us bail.

This insanity must end soon
while there is still something left
of the freedom in this country
that the world once thought was best!

— Syracuse, Prisoner of the Drug War

Federal Corrections Institute Dublin California, 1995

II
America's War at Home

The Drug War is America's longest war, and the first war fought on US soil since the Civil War. Strangely, it is not a war to fend off a foreign invasion, but a war directed against its citizens by a government claiming to act in the 'compelling' interests of society.

With an enormous budget to disperse among a myriad of government and advertising agencies, the Drug War is being fought in every neighborhood in this country, in the schools, the workplace, in the courts, in the media — it is pervasive, with no end in sight.

Begun as a moralistic crusade against a segment of the population who has fallen on the 'wrong' side of a somewhat arbitrary delineation between legal and illegal drugs, it has evolved into a huge industry that thrives on the doctrine of zero tolerance. Anyone who strays to the wrong side will be punished to the fullest extent of the law, with politicians ever ready to show their 'toughness' against this so-called threat to 'traditional American values'. In this type of system, compassion is interpreted as weakness. In its course towards a 'drug-free' America, this crusade sees the human right to political tolerance as its enemy. There is no room for the free and open discussion that Americans value or for an honest evaluation of the effectiveness of such a politicized drug policy: Zero tolerance prohibits any such consideration. There can be no discussion of root causes of crime and the drug problem, such as the social and economic ills of poverty, racism, exclusion, injustice or lack of treatment options.

Though the War on Drugs was first called for by Richard Nixon during his law and

General Barry McCaffrey serves as the nation's Director of the Office of National Drug Control Policy, or 'drug czar".

He is responsible for setting the nation's drug policy and determining the Drug War budget.

order candidacy for president in 1968, it became a real war during Ronald Reagan's presidency. Reagan enabled the military to be used for the first time in a century on domestic soil. Acts of war were enacted, providing law enforcement agencies and the criminal justice system with the ability to go after and mete out harsh punishments to prisoners, and for more prisons to accommodate America's Drug War POWs.

Nancy Reagan outlined the extremist position of the Reagan administration when she said, "There is no moral middle ground. Indifference is not an option. ... We want you to help us create an outspoken intolerance for drug use." Ronald Reagan's alcohol-drinking, nicotine-addicted drug czar, William Bennett, further limited the debate by labeling drug users as bad, dangerous people with corrupt values who must be 'weeded out' in the interests of society.

By dehumanizing a large segment of soci-

William with his wife, Susan, and their daughters, Danielle and Olivia.

William Stonner

age 40, serving 10 years

charged with manufacturing marijuana

---

ety and scapegoating 'druggies', this policy rationalized 'drug user profiles,' drug sweeps through neighborhoods, arbitrary drug testing of people in the workplace, and other systematic forms of oppression. Such scapegoating and intolerance fed an hysteria leading to LA Police Chief Daryl Gates' sincere suggestion to the Senate in 1990 that casual users "should be taken out and shot."

Human lives are not the only casualties of the Drug War. Our civil liberties and freedoms are, also. Rather than stand up for the Constitution, the US Supreme Court has facilitated the erosion of Fourth and Fifth Amendment protections of privacy and self-incrimination by allowing search and seizure, no-knock search warrants, and mandatory drug tests that do not identify addiction or impairment but merely track certain substances in the human body or excretions. It has also failed to protect our citizens' Sixth Amendment protection against secret witnesses. Asked to affirm Eighth amendment protections against unreasonable bail, the Court instead decided that drug suspects, even non-violent ones, can be denied those rights. Police and prosecutors have usurped

the power to determine punishment as well as to enforce laws. Perhaps, as the slogan suggests, it's a matter of "Free America or Drug-free America — you can't have both."

Are Americans willing to sacrifice all their liberties in the name of the Drug War? How did we get to this point?

The roots of prohibition

The federal government had no regulatory role in the drug trade until 1906, when labeling requirements were placed on patent medicines. In 1914 the Harrison Narcotics Act empowered the Narcotics Division of the IRS to issue tax stamps, keep records, and collect revenue on opium and coca products sold interstate.

Prohibition had been attempted and repeatedly ruled unconstitutional until 1919, when the 18th Amendment was passed. The violent and corrupt 'Roaring Twenties' began when the Volstead Act banned commerce in alcohol. It took Americans just over a decade to realize that Prohibition created more problems than it solved. The evidence was clear.

Gangs were selling liquor and fighting over their turf in the black market. There were drive-by shootings. Normally law-abiding citizens defied the laws and became criminals. Sound familiar?

People soon realized their mistake and adopted the 21st Amendment, repealing the only Constitutional authority that ever existed for prohibition. Harry Anslinger, the head of Prohibition enforcement, in a grab for power and job security, shifted to narcotics enforcement and actively lobbied Congress to criminalize a variety of legitimate activities.

In 1937, Anslinger engineered passage of the prohibitive Marihuana Tax Act. It was passed to crack down on Mexican-Americans, reefer-smoking Negroes, jazz musicians, and 'Hindoos' from Asia, as well as to secure the financial profits of DuPont and other petrochemical and timber interests who were threatened by new technical developments using the hemp plant.

The United Nations adopted the Single Convention Treaty on Narcotic Drugs in 1961, paving the way for harsh international enforcement.

Candidate Richard Nixon called for 'law and order' and declared 'War on Drugs' in 1968, stating "Public Enemy #1 in the US is drug abuse. In order to fight and defeat this enemy, it is necessary to wage a new, all-out offensive." In 1970, the US Controlled Substances Act was devised to create a formula by which drugs were 'scheduled' into various categories. This included a class of banned 'dangerous' substances. As president, he appointed the National Commission on Marihuana and Other Drugs, which looked into his idea, then recommended in 1972 that cannabis be decriminalized. Nixon refused to do so, declaring his 'moral' opposition to drugs. The drug scheduling process was made the sole discretion of the Drug Enforcement Agency, or DEA, in 1973. With Nixon's resignation in 1974 under a cloud of crimes and coverups, the Drug War stalled. Marijuana decriminalization gained a foothold.

On August 2, 1978, President Jimmy Carter publicly called on Congress to decriminalize marijuana in his statement on drug policy. But soon the hardliners reasserted themselves by changing research priorities, and banning references to 'responsible drug use' and 'use versus abuse' from federal publications. The national dialogue was again being narrowed.

> **"Since the use of marijuana and other narcotics is widespread among members of the New Left, you should be alert to opportunities to have them arrested by local authorities on drug charges."** — *J. Edgar Hoover, 1968*

Beverly (left) with her daughter Tymisha.

In their own words

Beverly Powell

age 42, serving 22 years
charged with with conspiracy to possess with intent to distribute cocaine base/cocaine

"This is supposed to be America, the country where there's liberty and justice for all. I'm not saying that I should not be punished for my crime, but 22 years for a first time, non-violent offender is cruel and inhuman punishment. The federal government is saying I don't deserve a second chance. This lock everyone up and throw away the key is something you hear about in other countries."

The politics of punishment

During the Reagan era in the 1980s, a growing fear of gangs, drugs, guns and violence led to a media outcry to address the crime problem. The Democratic House, struggling to overcome charges of being 'soft on crime,' responded with the Comprehensive Crime Control Act of 1984. This Act marked a shift toward harsher penalties for drug offenders. It included the most far-reaching modification of federal sentencing — the Sentencing Reform Act. The implementation and enforcement of these Acts were a turning point in the Drug War, resulting in the massive arrests of non-violent drug offenders and the subsequent massive growth in the prison population that we are experiencing today.

Federal sentencing disparities had been a concern for Congress, the criminal justice community, and the public for a long time. Indeterminate sentencing enabled judges to apply vastly different penalties to people charged with the same offense. There was a clear need for some structure and reform.

With the goals of reducing unwarranted disparities, increasing certainty and uniformity, and correcting "past patterns of undue leniency for certain categories of serious offenses," the 1984 Sentencing Reform Act created a permanent, independent agency within the judicial branch of government to formulate national sentencing guidelines with defined parameters for federal judges to follow in their sentencing decisions.

This independent agency, the US Sentencing Commission, was organized in 1985 to set the appropriate types and lengths of sentences for more than 2,000 different federal offenses. At the same time, Congress eliminated parole to ensure that "sentences pronounced would be sentences served." Judicial discretion in sentencing was vastly curtailed when these guidelines went into effect in 1987.

Meanwhile, 1986 was an election year, and drugs were in the headlines of all American papers, with crack cocaine getting the most media attention. The cocaine-related deaths of athletes Len Bias and Don Rogers within one week of each other fed a media frenzy that set Congress into motion. Within a month, Democratic Speaker of the House Tip O'Neill spearheaded passage of the Anti-Drug Abuse Act of 1986. This Act established a new set of non-parolable Mandatory Minimum Sentences (MMS) for drug offenses that affixed a minimum penalty to the amount of drugs involved. It sought to subject mid- and high-level drug dealers to five, ten, and twenty year sentences. This included first-time offenders.

Congress did not stop there. The 1988 Omnibus Anti-Drug Abuse Act continued to target different aspects of drug activity. Congress created a five year mandatory minimum for simple possession of more than five grams of 'crack' cocaine; much more severe than other drug possession charges. In addition, Congress doubled the existing ten year MMS to twenty years for an offender engaged in a Career Criminal Enterprise (CCE, an ongoing offense spanning a period of time). Perhaps most significant was the inclusion of conspiracy in the mandatory sentencing scheme. Although co-conspirators have different levels of involvement in drug trafficking conspiracies, this increased the likelihood that penalties would be applied equally to low- or mid-level participants as to the major dealers or 'king-pins.'

Under President George Bush, the full force of these sentencing reform schemes were felt. In 1989 US Attorney General Richard Thornburgh issued his infamous 'Thornburgh memorandum,' requiring all

---

"The punishment of large numbers of a nation's population is generally considered to be a regrettable status either reflective of a crime problem that has not been controlled through more pro-active interventions and/ or an indication of a society which imposes harsher sanctions than are felt necessary by other nations."
— Marc Mauer, The Sentencing Project, 1997

Hamedah Ali Hasan

**age 31, serving
LIFE without parole**

**charged with conspiracy to
distribute cocaine/cocaine base,
interstate travel in the aid of
racketeering, and use of a
telephone to commit a felony**

*"I was not willing to lie
for the 'deal'."*

**Hamedah, wearing head covering, with
her daughters, Kasaundra, Kamyra,
and Ayesha.**

Hamedah Ali Hasan's instructors in the Steps to Success Program attest that she was an impressive student with lots of promise. She was poised to make a decent life for herself and her three daughters, and felt like she was ready to seek employment with her exceptional skills. Unfortunately, she never got the chance to prove herself.

Instead, Hamedah sits in prison facing a life sentence for a crime she says she did not commit. She has no prior criminal or arrest history. She was never observed doing anything illegal related to the offenses for which she has been convicted.

Shortly after her arrest, she was offered immunity (all charges dropped) in exchange for her 'cooperation' with the US Attorney in obtaining a conviction against her cousin. She had no knowledge of the offenses and was not willing to lie for the 'deal.'

The evidence presented against her at the trial consisted primarily of hearsay testimony from alleged co-conspirators who directly benefitted either by getting immunity themselves or by testifying in exchange for a possible sentence reduction if they were currently in prison.

"My experience has clearly shown me that almost any violation of the law is excusable as long as the accused 'cooperates' with government attorneys and/or officials."

Amy's Story

Amy Pofahl

age 37, serving 24 years

charged with conspiracy to import and distribute MDMA (ecstasy), money laundering

Serving time for her ex-husband's crime

Amy with her Dad and Mom.

Amy's husband was Charles "Sandy" Pofahl, a graduate of Stanford Law School, successful Dallas businessman, and twenty years her senior. They were married for a few years, until she could no longer handle his alcohol problem.

In 1989, they had been separated for a year and Amy had her own promotional company, Prime Time, in Los Angeles, when her nightmare began. She found out that her estranged husband had been arrested in Germany for manufacturing and distributing ecstasy (MDMA). He mistakenly thought it was legal there at the time. Some of the ecstasy was traced to the US market.

Amy went about helping her husband out during his early confinement and trial. As a result, she also became a target of the US government. "Federal agents promised that if I refused to help them gain the information against my husband, they would destroy my life. This they did."

Friends and business clients of her thriving, new company were intimidated by agents. The agents told people that Amy was a drug dealer and associating with her would get them in trouble. Then, Amy was arrested and charged with conspiracy to commit the crimes previously attributed to her husband and his co-defendants. She was also accused of money laundering.

Amy refused to plea bargain or 'cooperate' in giving information that she didn't have. On top of that, she was misinformed about her rights by her court-appointed attorney, who failed to present certain evidence or call witnesses in her case, as she requested. Further, the prosecutor was able to move the trial to Waco, Texas where the judge's court was reputed to have a 100 percent conviction rate.

Her husband received a six year prison sentence in Germany, of which he served four. Incarcerated since 1991, Amy is still serving a 24-year sentence for his crimes.

"So much for keeping the streets free of criminals by demanding harsh mandatory minimums, because every single person who pled and was guilty in my case was handed his freedom in exchange for testimony.

"I can only speak for myself, but I am a witness to the type of women this drug war has attacked and victimized, and most do not belong in prison. If laws do not change, I will spend the majority of my adult life in prison. Is that fair to me, my family or the taxpayer? Who does it benefit? Please investigate my case and others. Visit a federal institution and witness for yourself who is filling these overcrowded prisons. You will be shocked. Please vote to change these unjust laws."

federal prosecutors to pursue the most severe charges possible in a case ... "the most serious readily provable offense or offenses consistent with the defendant's conduct." This vindictive policy ensured that MMS would pack the prisons with drug offenders.

Democrats and Republicans continue to vie to see who can be harsher at criminalizing and punishing people for illicit drugs.

In recent years, however, there has been a growing recognition by a cross-section of the American public, including judges, lawyers, wardens and law enforcement officers, that the drug laws have gone too far. Though the Sentencing Commission has continued to make recommendations to correct the most egregious disparities and injustices, politicians still refuse to support reform, afraid of being labeled 'soft on crime.'

Some relief has been found with the passage of the 1994 legislation called the 'safety valve.' This allows judges to deviate from the guidelines in cases of first-time, non-violent offenders, averting the application of harsh punishment in certain cases. But this legislation is not applied retroactively, so it leaves many first-timers in prison awaiting relief from long sentences that might not be given to them today.

Most modern societies hold the death penalty to be a human rights violation. The US is one of the few states with an accelerating execution rate. A few nations — ones that are notorious for human rights abuses, like China and Singapore — are disproportionately high in executions, and put to death those accused of drug offenses. America is poised to join their ranks.

Kay Tanner

age 56, serving 10 years
charged with cocaine conspiracy

In their own words

"The night before Christmas Eve, my front door was rammed in and approximately fifteen fully armed DEA and police invaded my home.

"This was all related to my tenants that had moved. I was handcuffed and interrogated for eight hours about people I didn't even know. I was threatened with arrest and they tore my house apart looking for evidence. I was not arrested as they found nothing they were looking for.

"I was later indicted for one count of Conspiracy to Traffic Cocaine. Conspiracy does not require any evidence. All you need is testimony by a government witness, which is bought with plea bargains. There were two witnesses who faced twenty year sentences and got only 12–18 months for their testimony. I was convicted for having knowledge of my tenants actions by hearsay only.

"I have lost my home and spent all of my money defending myself, trying to undo this nightmare.

"Prison is about loneliness and despair. About mothers and grandmothers without their families, most of which were victims themselves. Victims of their husbands, boyfriends or poorly chosen friends. Now they are victims of the federal government with no hope in sight.

The US 1994 federal crime bill included for the first time capital punishment for non-violent crimes, including some drug activities (see chart), based on a mathematical formula. It was signed into law by President Bill Clinton.

The Supreme Court has held that the death penalty is unconstitutional in cases that do not involve killing, striking down the death penalty in the case of rape. Whether this court would continue to follow its precedents is an open question, but at this point it is fair to say that these penalties are unconstitutional.

'One size fits all' penalties

If justice is to be served, the punishment must fit the crime. However, politicians have constructed bizarre sentencing schemes that defy all logic. Sentences of 189 years are meted out for charges based on hearsay rather than hard proof. Three life sentences were handed to Danielle Metz for her husband's crimes and a ten-year sentence was given to Nicole Richardson, who answered the phone and told someone a phone number.

It has become a 'one-size fits all' system that strips an individual from the context of his or her offense.

Such a system breeds unfairness — where non-violent drug offenders sit in prison and watch child abusers, murderers, and rapists released before they are.

THE DEATH PENALTY FORMULA

841(b)(1)(B) quantity X 600 = (Amount for MMS of 5 years)	Death Penalty Net quantity
100 grams heroin	60 kilograms
500 g cocaine	300 kg
5 g crack	3 kg
10 g PCP (pure)	6 kg
100 g PCP (mixture)	60 kg
100 kg of marijuana	60,000 kg
100 marijuana plants	60,000 plants*
10 g methamphetamine (pure)	6 kg
100 g meth (mixture)	60 kg

Source: Criminal Justice Policy Foundation

* Non-psychoactive, industrial hemp is typically grown at a seeding rate of more than 600,000 plants per acre. The law makes no distinction between hemp and marijuana.

Punishments for first-time drug offenses, compared with certain other offenses

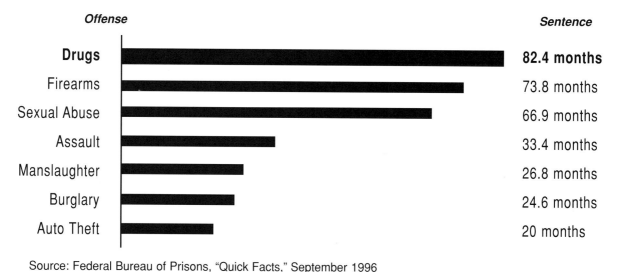

Offense		Sentence
Drugs		**82.4 months**
Firearms		73.8 months
Sexual Abuse		66.9 months
Assault		33.4 months
Manslaughter		26.8 months
Burglary		24.6 months
Auto Theft		20 months

Source: Federal Bureau of Prisons, "Quick Facts," September 1996

Danielle with her son, Carl, and daughter, Glennisha.

Danielle Metz

age 31, serving 3 LIFE sentences + 20 years

charged with conspiracy to distribute cocaine,
continuing criminal enterprise,
money laundering

"When I was arrested these people told me that they didn't want me for anything that they wanted my husband and if I would tell them everything that they needed to know that I would be set free and if I couldn't I would never see my kids again. I replied by saying that I couldn't tell them what I did not know."

Conspiracy law: Thought crime

How broadly has the Drug War's net been cast? You never have to touch any drugs or money to be prosecuted in the Drug War. It's what you know or don't know; it's who you know, or what somebody else says you did. That's the mechanism behind conspiracy laws, which often carry the longest sentences of any crime. Consider Amy Pofahl, serving 24 years for her ex-husband's crimes.

The drug conspiracy law is not like the general federal conspiracy law, applicable in non-drug cases such as murder, which requires proof not only of the conspiracy, but that an overt act "to effect the object of the conspiracy" actually occurred. By contrast, drug conspiracy law provides simply that "any person who attempts or conspires to commit" a drug crime is guilty of conspiracy and subject to the same penalties as those who carry out the offense. In 1994, in an opinion written by Justice Sandra Day O'Connor, the US Supreme Court unanimously ruled that conspiring to commit a narcotics crime can be a violation of Federal law even if the conspiracy is never carried out. So just talking about breaking a drug law is enough to earn a decades-long prison sentence.

People with no active participation in a drug offense are penalized for 'aiding and abetting' simply for knowing about a situation and not reporting it to the police. They can even be sentenced for not knowing about a plan or situation prosecutors say they should have known about, and some even have been arrested for trying to talk someone out of committing a drug crime!

You can be sentenced because someone who committed a crime is pressured to give your name and testify against you as the only way to get their own sentence reduced or have their charges dropped. A paid informant may snitch on you just to make some spending money. No corroborating evidence is required. In fact, no crime need be committed. Someone just has to mention the idea of a crime in your presence.

> **"Penalties against possession of a drug should not be more damaging to an individual than the use of the drug itself."**
> **— *President Jimmy Carter***
> Statement to Congress, August 2, 1978

The Tuckers' Story

Upper right: Joanne Tucker.

Above: Steve (2nd from left) and Gary Tucker (right) visited by their brother, Kenny (left) and their mother, Doris Gore.

Joanne Tucker
serving 10 years

Gary Tucker
serving 16 years

Steve Tucker
age 46, serving 10 years

Charged with conspiracy to manufacture marijuana; Conspiracy to "knowingly know" that others are growing marijuana

By July, 1992, the DEA was involved in Operation Green Merchant, a campaign to eradicate indoor marijuana cultivation across the USA.

Their targets were hydroponics stores and their customers all over the country. They would copy down the license plate numbers of customers, follow and spy on them, steal their garbage, and subpoena utility bills to check for high electrical usage.

Out of Operation Green Merchant grew Operation Triox. This time their target was a small, hydroponics store called Southern Lights and Hydroponics, Inc. in Norcross, Georgia. The owner, Gary Tucker, was approached by the DEA to put cameras in this store to secretly film all of his customers. His refusal to cooperate led to a promise to

shut him down. The feds did more than that before they were done.

Gary Tucker, his wife Joanne, and his brother Steven, were convicted of conspiracy to manufacture marijuana based on the offenses of a few of their customers, with whom they had no contact beyond selling equipment that is completely legal.

The Tuckers had no marijuana on their person, in their homes, or in their store. Nor did they have any drug paraphernalia. They were never caught selling or buying drugs.

Gary Tucker wrote, "My main concern is that America is becoming a police state — that we are losing our liberties and the politicians are using the drug war as an excuse."

Loren Pogue

age 64, serving 22 years

charged with conspiracy to import drugs and money laundering

"It takes only two hours to destroy your life"

Loren with his grandchild.

Helping his part-time employee close a sale of land in Costa Rica has sent Loren Pogue, real estate agent, missionary, former serviceman, Mason, Shriner, Lions Club Member, American Legion, VFW, and past Director of Children's Home, to prison for 22 years. He was an unsuspecting victim of a reverse sting operation.

As it turned out, his employee was a paid government informer, to the tune of $250,000.00. The informant pleaded with Loren to help him sell a plot of land on a Costa Rican mountainside to a group posing as "investors" — in reality, they were undercover agents who were shopping for a place to build an airstrip. Pogue never saw nor spoke with the undercover agents prior to the one meeting he had with them.

That Pogue was an upstanding member of the community, that he had no drug history; that the airstrip was never built; and that, even if built, it would be useless because of its location; none of this played any part in the court's decision.

Loren has 15 adopted children. He went "in a two hour meeting from a happy, joyful life to pain, hurt and suffering." His family cannot afford to visit him because he is being held 1500 miles away.

"There were no drugs involved. The government agents said they were going to fly 1000 kilos of drugs into the US and that is what I was sentenced on."

As Judge Jack D. Shanstrom explains in his instructions to the jury in Jodie Israel's marijuana conspiracy trial:

"An overt act does not itself have to be unlawful. A lawful act may be an element of a conspiracy if it was done for the purpose of carrying out the conspiracy. The government is not required to prove that the defendant personally did one of the overt acts. Once you have decided that the defendant was a member of a conspiracy, the defendant is responsible for what other conspirators said or did to carry out the conspiracy, whether or not the defendant knew what they said or did."

The judge continued, "Instruction 47: A defendant's knowledge of and participation in a conspiracy may be inferred from circumstantial evidence and from evidence of the defendant's actions. Acts which seem otherwise innocent, when viewed in the context of the surrounding circumstances may justify an inference of complicity."

With this logic, no one is safe — except government agents, who are paid to go into society and manufacture, buy, sell and use illegal drugs, propose and arrange drug deals, and commit all manner of crimes to entrap others. The end result is that we are incarcerating a growing number of people for events that may or may not even have occurred.

Mandatory Minimums

Mandatory Minimum Sentences (MMS) for drugs are based on these factors: the type of drug, weight of the drug, and a person's criminal history. In addition, a five year mandatory minimum can be triggered by the presence of a weapon at a crime scene.

Dubbed the "law of unintended consequence" by US Supreme Court Justice William Rhenquist, MMS have not provided the results that were originally intended — to eliminate drugs from the streets by keeping 'kingpins' and mid-level drug dealers behind bars for a long time. To the contrary, reports show that America's drug supply has not been substantially reduced, and studies conclude that it is the low-level minor participant rather than the kingpin who is bearing the brunt of the law.

Many judges have complained that MMS 'tie their hands' and do not allow them to view each case on its own terms. In effect, MMS have shifted judicial discretion to the prosecutors. It is the prosecutor who decides what quantity of drugs to charge, whether a plea bargain will be offered, if a defendant's 'cooperation' will be rewarded or denied, and what the sentence will be. The judge's job is to merely 'rubber stamp' the prosecutor's determination.

Federal Mandatory Minimums for First-time Drug Offenders*

Drug Charge Type of Substance	5 Years No parole	10 Years No parole
LSD	1 gram	10 grams
Marijuana	100 plants/ 100 kilos	1000 plants/ 1000 kilos
Crack Cocaine	5 grams	50 grams
Powder Cocaine	500 grams	5 kilos
Heroin	100 grams	1kilo
Methamphetamine	10 grams	100 grams

Other Mandatory Sentences
(added to sentence)

Offense	Sentence
Armed Career Criminal Act (Felon in possession of a gun)	15 years
Continuing Criminal Enterprise	20 years
Possession of a gun during a drug offense	5 years

* Prisoners must serve at least 85% of the sentence

Mandatory Minimum Sentences were first introduced for drug offenses in the 1950s as the Boggs Act. Within 20 years, they were repealed as Congress realized that they failed to reduce drug use, inhibited judicial flexibility, and overflowed the prisons.

'Shomari' Stanley Huff

age 56, serving 15 years

charged with trafficking a half-kilo of crack cocaine

Stanley with his sons, Quentin and Xavier.

"Today a friend and I sat down and made a list of all the men and women that have been charged or sentenced under federal drug laws for 'crack.' We came up with 48 names, all black.

"We went back to Oct. '94 and just this one jail. Not one white has graced these portals with a crack cocaine charge (federal, that is).

"I'm working on a claim of 'selective prosecution' by the federal government. The majority of us were charged with violation of Minnesota State Statutes. After about a month, the Feds step in and file federal charges.

"Creating 'selective prosecution' laws that affect one race over another is so unconstitutional as to reek of the stench that slavery held for so many years. This should be brought to the attention of the people on a national level."

Judges are not allowed to consider any of the following factors:

• The nature and circumstances of the offense

• The history and character of the defendant

• The motivation to break the law

• The role of the offender in the offense

• The likelihood of the person to re-offend

• Alternative sentencing options

Meanwhile, the person convicted of a drug offense must serve 85 percent of the designated sentence. The penalties are rigid and unyielding.

As Judge Franklin Billings said, it denies judges "the right to bring their conscience, experience, discretion and sense of what is just into the sentencing procedure, and it, in effect, makes a judge a computer, automatically imposing sentences without regard to what is right and just."

The only way a judge can reduce an MMS is if the defendant cooperates or provides "substantial assistance" in prosecuting someone else, otherwise known as 'snitching' on a husband, family member, or friend. If you have no information to trade, you are out of luck. Unlike the organizer, the minor player seldom has valuable information to trade for a lower sentence. US District Judge Terry Hatter, Jr. summarized the situation: "The people at the very bottom who can't provide substantial assistance end up getting [punished] more severely than those at the top."

MMS are racially discriminatory

Mandatory minimums are discriminatory in application, creating racially-based sentencing disparities.

Studies show that Blacks and Hispanics are more likely to receive MMS than whites charged with the same crime. In addition, the Federal Judicial Center found that Blacks received sentences that were 28 percent longer than whites.

Mandatory minimum prison sentences are structurally discriminatory. It takes 100 times more cocaine in powder form than crack form to receive a MMS, despite the fact that the two drugs are almost identical, both in terms of chemistry and physiological effects. Undercover DEA agents have actually exploited this distinction and forced dealers to cook powder cocaine into crack in order to ensure a lengthier MMS.

Crack is cheaper than the powder, making it more affordable to people in inner city communities. While white Americans show higher rates of crack use than Blacks, African Americans are serving 88 percent of the prison sentences for crack offenses.

Christmas behind bars for Johnny Patillo and his children on visiting day. A fellow inmate portrays Santa Claus.

Johnny Patillo

serving 10 years

charged with shipping a Fed Ex package of crack cocaine for a friend

MMS are arbitrary and unfair

Possession of 4.99 grams of crack can be punishable with no more than one year in prison; but possession of 5.01 grams of crack by a first-time offender must be sentenced to a mandatory minimum of five years. These 'sentencing cliffs', as they are known, create absurd disparities in sentencing, yet there is no way for judges to circumvent them.

Furthermore, because of the way the law is written, a drug is defined as any mixture that contains the drug, resulting in even more absurd sentences. For instance, mandatory minimums for LSD are calculated using the weight of the carrier medium, such as blotter paper. Depending on the carrier (liquid, blotter paper, or gels), the sentence for 1,000 doses can range from fifteen months to thirty years. As a result of the sentencing formula, the accused may serve more time in prison for the weight of the carrier than for the actual drug on it.

In one judge's words

Reagan appointee Judge J. Spencer Letts, US District Court of Central District of California, wrote these passages in his sentencing memorandum on Johnny Patillo:

"Statutory mandatory minimum sentences create injustice because the sentence is determined without looking at the particular defendant....

"Under 21 USC S.841 (b) (1) (A), the mandatory minimum sentence is triggered by two factors only: (1) the type of drug and (2) the amount of drug.

"In this case, it is the fact that the package defendant brought to Federal Express contained 681 grams of crack cocaine which raises this offense to one in which the minimum sentence is ten years, without the possibility of parole. If the package contained a different narcotic, or a lesser quantity of the same substance, defendant might have been sentenced to straight parole.

"The minimum ten year sentence to be served by defendant was determined by Congress before he ever committed a criminal act. Congress decided to hit the problem of drugs, as they saw it, with a sledgehammer, making no allowance for the circumstances of any particular case. Under this sledgehammer approach, it can make no difference whether defendant actually owned the drugs with which he was caught, or whether, at a time when had an immediate need for cash, he was suckered into taking the risk of being caught with someone else's drugs.

"Under the statutory minimum, it can make no difference whether he is a lifetime criminal or a first time offender. Indeed, under this sledgehammer approach, it could make no difference if the day before making his one slip in an otherwise unblemished life, defendant had rescued fifteen children from a burning building, or had won the Congressional Medal of Honor while defending his country. …

"Since the days when amputation of the offending hand was routinely used as the punishment for stealing a loaf of bread one of the basic precepts of criminal justice has been that the punishment fit the crime.

"This is the principle which, as a matter of law, I must violate in this case."

MMS are socially costly

With so much talk in Congress about 'Family Values,' one might expect to see some concern about the destruction of the family unit caused by the Drug War; the human damage done to those imprisoned for unduly long periods of time, and to their families. Marriages are difficult to sustain over a ten to twenty year separation due to incarceration.

The national Judicial Conference of the United States, the special Federal Courts Study Committee, twelve Federal Circuit Courts, and the American Bar Association have all called for the repeal of mandatory sentences.
— Families Against Mandatory Minimums

Perry holding photos of his children.

Perry Adron McCullough

serving 189 years, 8 months
charged with conspiracy to transport cocaine

"I received 189 years, eight months for a first-time, non-violent, victimless, consensual transaction with another adult.

"The only 'evidence' against me was the testimony of a four-time convicted felon facing two indictments for drug dealing. He would have gotten 'life imprisonment without the possibility of parole' but as a reward for giving the prosecutor me, he received a five year sentence."

Parents must sacrifice the role of raising their own children.

The Drug War will take the family's breadwinner, throw him in prison, seize their home, car and savings, and throw the family onto the welfare rolls, or take both parents and force the children to fend for themselves, to live with relatives or in separate or foster homes. Such collateral damage imposed by MMS is not calculated into the punishment given to the drug offender.

MMS are financially costly

• The Department of Justice budget has grown 162 percent since the enactment of mandatory minimums in 1987, compared to the Department of Education budget of only 77 percent. (Bureau of Justice Statistics, 1995).

• The Federal Bureau of Prisons budget has grown 1,400 percent since the enactment of mandatory minimums in 1987. The budget jumped from $220 million in 1986 to $3.19 billion in 1997. (*Bureau of Justice Statistics Sourcebook*, National Drug Control Strategy.)

Each year, the portion of your tax dollars that goes to support federal prisoners grows faster than any other federal expenditure, including education, defense, the environment, transportation and social security.

State sentencing laws

Sentencing options vary greatly, depending on which jurisdiction prosecutes a case, the federal government or a state. The same drug offense that could put someone on probation in one state could bring a five-year sentence in a federal prison, or a life sentence in another state.

Certain states, like Oklahoma or Texas, are notorious for issuing extremely harsh sentences for small quantities of drugs. Melinda George was sentenced in the State of Texas to

---

Valerie Johnson

age 33, serving 10 years, 1 month

charged with possession with intent to distribute crack cocaine

"I was charged as a first-time offender. I have been given 121 months and five years supervised release for only 87.8 grams of cocaine base. If I would have been charged with just cocaine I would have gotten 24 months.

"When I was in one prison, I had a roommate who killed her daughter and she is doing less time than me — a non-violent, low-level offender.

"That bothers me.

"My grandmother, 74, said to me the other day, 'Baby, you can tell me what you really did, we'll still love you.' They think I killed someone or something. It's so hard to explain this to them, they just don't understand.

"It's just not fair. "

99 years for charges revolving around a tenth of a gram of cocaine. The State of Louisiana has a mandatory sentence of life without parole for manufacture or distribution of any amount of crack cocaine or possession of any amount of heroin.

If the cases of James Geddes and Will Foster had been tried in California rather than Oklahoma, chances are they would be given probation rather than the ninety-plus year sentences they received for marijuana cultivation. If Foster had been charged under California law after the passage of Proposition 215, which allows marijuana cultivation for medical purposes, his charges might have been dismissed altogether. Still, California has a very high rate of incarceration, with more inmates in its state prisons (155,000) than are in the entire federal prison system.

About forty states now have some mandatory minimums on their books. New York passed its "Rockefeller Laws" in 1973, requiring minimums of fifteen years for possession or sale of four or more ounces of hard (pharmaceutical) drugs.

In 1978, Michigan enacted its '650-lifer law' which requires mandatory life imprisonment for possession, sales, or conspiracy to sell or possess 650 grams (about 1-1/4 pounds) of heroin or cocaine. Only people convicted of first degree murder get the same sentence. Although the law was claimed to have been intended to target the big king-pins, it has not worked this way. Eighty-six percent of those who received life were first-time offenders.

Former Michigan Governor William G. Milliken recently admitted that he made a mistake in signing the '650-lifer' law twenty years ago. He said the law is "inhumane", and "wastes precious public dollars to lock up for life people who pose no threat to society." He said the people who are locked up under this law would be "better served by treatment than prison."

Veronica with her daughter.

Veronica Flournoy

age 31, serving 8 years to Life
charged with sale of heroin and
possession of cocaine
sentenced under NY Rockefeller laws

- **Today 70% of all women incarcerated in New York prisons were convicted of non-violent drug law violations.**

- **95% of women sentenced under the Rockefeller Drug Laws have no prior criminal history.**

- **Approximately 23% of state prisoners are drug offenders.**

  — *JusticeWorks Community*

Melinda George

age 27, serving 99 years

**charged with sale of
1/10 gram of cocaine**

State of Texas

"I pray someone will show me some mercy and give me a second chance at life. I'd like to have children someday."

Remember Me
by Melinda George

*Prison's no place for an innocent child
There's no room for the meek,
no room for the mild.*

*The nights are so lonely I toss in my bed
The days are so dreary
I face them with dread.*

*Grant me one prayer as you did from the cross
For that thief who knew that his life was a loss.*

*Please come to this prison where I sit alone
Surrounded by razor wire, guard towers,
and stone.*

*Broken and penitent, forgotten and lost
on the ash heap of regret where my life
was tossed.*

*I've no other place left on this earth
Remember me O' Lord! Renew me by birth.*

*Come to this prison, enter my cell
Save me, forgive me, in this man-made hell.*

*And if in this life, no home here I see
In your Kingdom of Forgiveness, Lord, please
Remember me!*

Universal Declaration of Human Rights, Article 5.

"No one shall be subjected to torture or to cruel, inhuman or degrading treatment or punishment."

James' Story

James Geddes

age 47, serving 90 years

charged with cultivation and possession of five marijuana plants

State of Oklahoma

James Geddes, right, with his brother and mother.

In 1992, James Geddes was walking along a street with a friend when he got arrested. The police got a search warrant and went to the home rented by his friend. They found a small amount of marijuana, paraphernalia for smoking marijuana, and five plants growing in their vegetable garden.

There was no evidence that James lived at this house, although he was a frequent visitor.

James refused to plea bargain as he claimed his innocence and was sentenced to 75 years and one day for cultivation of five plants and to another 75 years, plus one day for possession of marijuana, for a total of 150 years and one day.

He was also charged with possession of a firearm and paraphernalia.

James filed an appeal on his disproportionate sentence. In 1995, his appeal came through, which reduced it to 90 years.

"I honestly feel like I have been kidnapped by the state of Oklahoma. I have never murdered anyone, raped anyone, or hurt any children. People feel they have the right to choose their sexual preference. If they want to end a life by abortion, if they want to inject nicotine into their lungs, if they want to drug themselves with alcohol, but because I choose to smoke a little marijuana, I have to go to prison for years, maybe the rest of my life....

"How can it be that the President, his wife, the Vice President and his wife, the mayor of Washington DC, even the Speaker of the House can do these things, but I must pay dearly?"

Three Strikes and You're Out

What you see is not always what you get, and that turned out to be the case in the states' "Three Strikes" laws. They double the sentence for a second felony offense, and give 25-years-to-life for the third. Drug possession by someone on parole is all it takes.

In March, 1996, the Justice Policy Institute reported that "more than twice as many pot smokers have been imprisoned under California's 'three strikes' law as murderers, rapists and kidnappers combined." By the beginning of 1996, state data showed that 3,749 people were imprisoned for drug possession under the law, compared to 2,432 defendants sentenced for all violent crimes.

This clogs the courts and feeds the need to build more prisons.

> **Between 1995 and the start of the current Drug War in 1985, the number of adults in prison has jumped 131%, the number in jail has doubled, on parole up by 134%, and the number on probation by 61%.**
>
> **— US Dept. of Justice.**

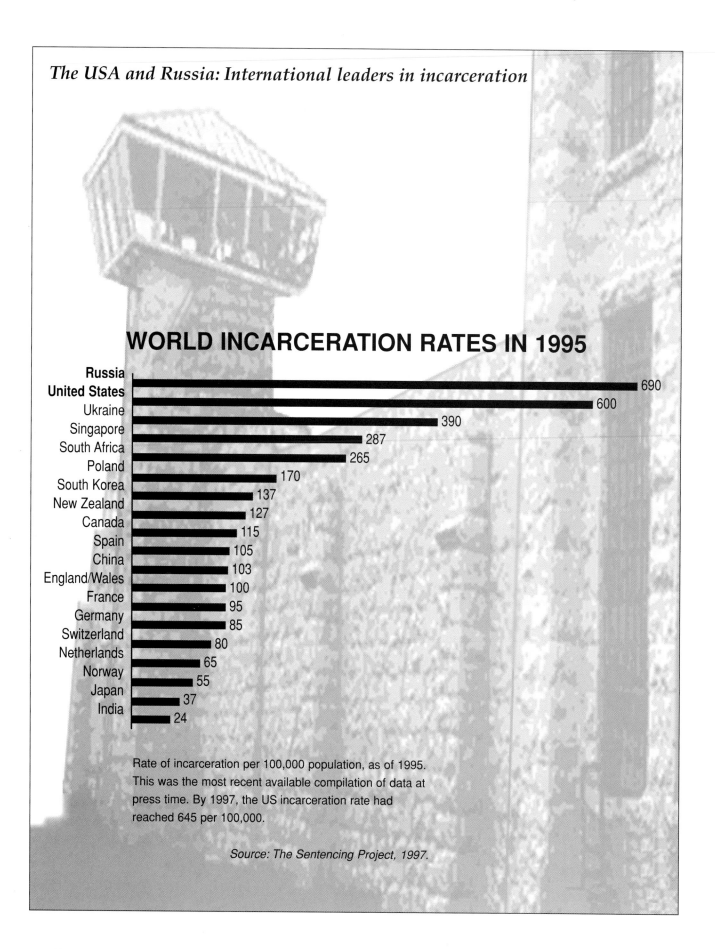

The USA and Russia: International leaders in incarceration

WORLD INCARCERATION RATES IN 1995

Country	Rate
Russia	690
United States	600
Ukraine	390
Singapore	287
South Africa	265
Poland	170
South Korea	137
New Zealand	127
Canada	115
Spain	105
China	103
England/Wales	100
France	95
Germany	85
Switzerland	80
Netherlands	65
Norway	55
Japan	37
India	24

Rate of incarceration per 100,000 population, as of 1995. This was the most recent available compilation of data at press time. By 1997, the US incarceration rate had reached 645 per 100,000.

Source: The Sentencing Project, 1997.

III.
The Prison Boom

The United States' incarceration rate is higher than at any other time in history. Driven by the Drug War, our proportional prison population is from six to ten times as high as most Western European nations.

Ironically, the sole exception is Russia — America's former adversary. Despite huge fiscal and human costs, both nations continue to post unacceptably high crime rates despite their record high rates of incarceration.

According to the Department of Justice, one out of 35 American adults were under the direct control of corrections agencies in 1996. That includes some 5.5 million people in jails, prisons, on probation or on parole — about 1.2 million in state or federal prison, 510,000 in jail, 3.8 million on probation and parole. There were 200,000 more prisoners in 1996 than in 1995.

As of June, 1997 there were 1.7 million inmates nationally. A Justice Department study said the odds that a newborn American will eventually go to prison now run one in 20. In a March, 1998 speech, the nation's drug czar, General Barry McCaffrey, referred to this as America's "internal gulag."

"We can't arrest our way out of this problem," McCaffrey said in a television interview, "We're willing to pay $23,000 a head to keep them in a cell. We've got to develop the political will to spend the money needed not only on prevention programs but on effective drug treatment in the criminal justice system and during follow-up care."

The general needs to live up to his words and not sidestep his role in changing the government's manner of dealing with the issue.

Nicole with her mother, Angela Hopkins.

Nicole Richardson

age 25, serving 10 years

charged with conspiracy to distribute LSD by providing a phone number to an acquaintance of her boyfriend

Filling America's prisons with drug offenders

The Drug War is largely responsible for the crisis of overcrowded prisons today, filling them with non-violent drug offenders.

In 1970, sixteen percent of federal prisoners were drug offenders. In 1998, the Federal Bureau of Prisons (BOP) reported that almost sixty percent (55,624) of the federal prison population, were serving time on drug offenses. Meanwhile, only 2.5 percent of inmates were incarcerated for violent offenses.

In state prisons, the Sentencing Project has estimated that 23 percent (about 243,700) of the million plus prisoners are drug offenders. Additionally, about 130,400 inmates are awaiting trial or serving time for a drug offense in local jails. Altogether, we are approaching a half-million American drug offenders languishing behind bars.

The chart below reflects only the federal prison profile. State and local information varies by locality.

Targeting minorities

Though the Drug War crosses all socioeconomic and color lines, an analysis of the general prison population reveals that most of the inmates are poor, undereducated males, and disproportionately persons of an ethnic minority. About 51 percent of state and federal inmates are African American and fifteen percent are Hispanic. The majority of them are serving time for non-violent property and drug crimes.

Almost one in three African American males (compared to one in eight Hispanics and one in fifteen whites) between the ages of

---

Federal Bureau of Prisons

United States Federal Prisoners Profile, 1998

Number of Institutions	93					
		SENTENCED IMPOSED****		INMATES BY SECURITY LEVEL		
TOTAL POPULATION*	116,376	Under 1 year	1.8%	Minimum	28.0%	
in BOP facilities**	105,090	1-3 years	12.8%	Low	35.1%	
in Contract facilities***	11,286	3-5 years	13.5%	Medium	23.0%	
		5-10 years	30.1%	High	13.8%	
AVERAGE INMATE AGE	37	10-15 years	20.1%			
		15-20 years	8.8%			
GENDER		20 years – Life	10.1%	PERSONNEL	30,208	
Male	93%	Life	2.8%			
Female	7%					
		TYPE OF OFFENSE ****				
RACE		**Drug offenses**	**59.1%**			
White	56.4%	Robbery	9.3%			
Black	40.3%	Extortion, Fraud,				
Asian	1.7%	Bribery	5.6%			
Native American	1.5%	Firearms, Explosives,				
		Arson	8.9%			
ETHNICITY		Property offenses	5.8%			
Hispanic	28.3%	**Violent offenses**	**2.5%**			
		Immigration	4.1%			
CITIZENSHIP		White Collar	0.7%			
United States	72.8%	Continuing Criminal				
Mexico	9.7%	Enterprises	0.8%			
Colombia	4.1%	Courts or Corrections	0.6%			
Cuba	2.7%	Miscellaneous	2.6%			
Other	10.7%	National Security	0.1%			

* Total sentenced and detained including all Bureau of Prison (BOP) facilities and contract facilities.

** Penitentiaries, Federal Correctional Institutions, Federal Prison Camps, Metropolitan Correctional Centers, Federal Medical Centers, and others.

*** Community Corrections Centers or detention facilities contracted by the BOP, operated by non-Bureau staff. The Bureau contracts with these facilities to house Federal offenders on a per capita basis.

**** Refers to sentenced offenders in BOP facilities.

March 28, 1998. For additional information, please contact the Prison Bureau's Office of Public Affairs at 202-307-3198.

twenty and 29 are currently under some form of criminal justice supervision — either in prison, on probation or on parole. If this trend continues, African American children will be more likely to go to prison than to a university when they grow up.

The Drug War is being fought in every neighborhood in America, urban and rural. Inner city neighborhoods with more visible street activity are particularly targeted. The introduction of crack cocaine in the 1980s has brought many problems to these already economically deprived communities. The opportunity for quick money has lured many into the drug trade. In some instances the lucrative underground market in drugs has led to an increase in violence and 'turf wars.' Calls from many within and outside of the neighborhoods to crack down on drug users and dealers have been met with 'neighborhood sweeps' by the police that include the rounding up of gang members, the elimination of 'crack houses,' and the arrest and prosecution of highly visible, street-level drug offenders.

According to criminal justice statistics, only fifteen percent of the nation's drug users are African American, yet they represent almost forty percent of all drug arrests and 55 percent of those convicted. This disparity raises questions about the disproportionate targeting of certain groups for prosecution, the impact of a lack of funds to pay for an adequate defense, and the unwillingness to address the root causes that are fueling these drug problems in the inner cities.

Given the reports of drug trafficking by federal officials, particularly in the CIA, many minority communities have come to regard

Everett with his wife, Brenda, and son, Everett, IV.

In their own words

Everett Gholston, III

age 40, serving 12 years, 7 mos.

charged with conspiracy to distribute cocaine

"Since I've been in prison, I've opened my eyes and mind and have really got a look at the outside world and our current government. Since being inside, I've seen the real impact of this war on drugs. I've realized that a lot of guys here are not bad people even though what they did and what I did was against the law and that was to sell drugs to make ends meet. Not to get rich, just to pay life's everyday bills like rent and utilities, car insurance and so on. I haven't met a real kingpin yet.

"I've realized that prisons are a business, factory behind fences, and a human warehouse. There's no real rehabilitation, job training, or schooling, and the little you do learn it will be so long before you get to practice your skills that you kind of lose interest. You know there's a light at the end of the tunnel, but it looks very dim.

"I've realized that drugs should be a medical issue and not a criminal issue and if the government keeps up the pace the black male and family will become extinct. I don't want to make this a race issue, because there are many white men here also, but just a few compared to the whole population in prison."

An African American is more than seven times as likely to be incarcerated as a white; nearly five times as likely as his South African counterpart!

Tonya Drake

age 35, serving 10 years

first offense, charged with possession with intent to distribute crack cocaine

"The feds have taken all my rights from me. They take a good person out of society for a mistake and leave the real crazy criminal out there free."

Tonya (left) with her children (l-r) Diona, Dion, Deisan, and Deidai.

In the summer of 1990, after working at several jobs ranging from waitress to secretary, Tonya Drake was trying to support her four young children on the benefits she received from AFDC, Aid to Families with Dependent Children.

That fateful day, June 21, Tonya attended a swap meet near her home in Inglewood, CA, where she ran into an acquaintance from her neighborhood, Fred Haley. He asked her to mail a present to his brother in Chicago because, he said, his birthday was the next day and it had to go out right away.

Haley handed her a $100 bill and said to keep the change. Tonya felt a little suspicious, but "I needed the money for my children, so I took the chance."

The security guard at the Airborne Express office also became suspicious because they rarely dealt with individuals at their airport location and because Tonya appeared "nervous." He followed her outside and took down her license plate, then he and other employees opened and searched the package to find a plastic bag inside a laundry soap box. The Los Angeles Police Department field test on the contents established them as 232 grams of crack cocaine.

When called in for questioning by the LAPD, Tonya, having no knowledge of the criminal justice system, told the above story. When her mandatory minimum sentence was handed down, however, she was ineligible for a "substantial assistance" reduction because Haley died shortly after her arrest. Federal agents took over the case because of the amount of drugs involved.

Tonya's children have fortunately been able to remain in the house they shared with Tonya's older sister and her family. She spends her time working in 'cut and sew' and attending night school and Jehovah's Witness services. Tonya prays "that Jehovah will answer my prayer to be back with my children so they won't make no mistakes like I did."

Michael Clarke

**age 28, serving 13 years
charged with possession with
intent to distribute crack cocaine**

*"I've never seen my son
as a free man."*

Michael with his son, Malik.

Michael Clarke had a promising future. He was a senior at North Carolina Central University, majoring in visual communication and art. He was engaged to be married to an intelligent woman who was also a student at the University of North Carolina at Chapel Hill.

They had great plans. Unfortunately, his family began having serious financial problems when his mother got injured while trying to send two sons to college. Michael took part-time jobs, "but that did not even put a dent in the problem." He was desperate and took the quick, easy way out. He began to sell crack.

Although his financial woes began to subside, other problems arose. His schoolwork and his relationship began to suffer. At his fiancee's urging, he quit. She was pregnant with his child, and they were close to graduating and reaching their dreams. But, then he got robbed, and the financial problems arose again. "The answer came wrapped in a beautifully packaged box with ignorance hiding inside with a one-way ticket to destruction," he wrote. He was

In 1997, the national unemployment rate was 5%. The rate for African American young men in inner cities was 30%.

arrested after two individuals set him up as "the sacrificial lamb."

"You want to know what's overwhelmingly painful; I've never seen my son as a free man.... I made a mistake, but my sentence is drastically exaggerated. My mistake is being used to stuff ballot boxes. It doesn't take thirteen years to realize that there are other legal ways to empower yourself financially.

"I'm optimistic about my future, but sometimes I can't help but to worry about the effects of each passing moment away from my son and the crust of time that becomes thicker and thicker sealing a distance between us.

"I have a little brother whose my co-defendant with 27 years who shouldn't even be in the system, but the system allows hearsay and lies to convict to fill their coffers. This is outrageous. Here I am an individual that has never been in any trouble before, not even a traffic ticket but yet I had to cop-out to thirteen years. This is not rehabilitation, this is production of hardened criminals, destruction of families. Suppression of the effects will not solve the root causes until the real causes are addressed. America will continue to fall into an infinite abyss.

"I'm a pawn in the game and I know this. I'm taking the fall for the 'Fat Cats' — those who import the drugs, those who allow the drugs to enter the country and those who hide behind bureaucracy. I own no plane, ship or any other radar-evasive vehicle. I'm at the bottom of the totem pole. I'm the effect, not the cause. I say 'Justice'."

Miguel (2nd from right) with friends and family.

Miguel Kercado

age 37, serving 20 years

charged with conspiracy to distribute heroin

Michael Brockett

age 42, serving Life

charged with conspiracy to distribute cocaine and crack cocaine

the government as hostile, at best, and as a possible source of many of these drugs. Credible reports have traced cocaine to the Iran / Contra scandal of the 1980s. When, in 1996, a major crack dealer claimed that the drug had been funneled by the CIA through his organization into the inner cities, it took more than a year for the CIA to rebut the allegations, and it did so without ever talking to the principle people making the charges against it. It is understandable that many African Americans do not trust such 'investigations' and denials by various government entities. Too many of their family members are in prison — but no CIA agents have been prosecuted or incarcerated for their drug activities and misconduct.

The high level of incarceration has had a serious impact on the African American community. It not only erodes the community's ability to participate in civic life when felony convictions take away people's right to vote, but it contributes to the further breakdown of the family.

The removal of Black men and women from the community imposes extra burdens on financially strapped family members who are left to take care of prisoners' children. If the grandmother or other extended family members are unable to provide care, then the breakdown of the African American family will be even more severe as the children become wards of the state and are placed in foster care.

The psychological effects and consequences to the community caused by the separation of parents and children and the incarceration of a significant portion of the population are obviously enormous.

Anger, bitterness and hopelessness, all derived from this systematic brutality, are manifest in detrimental ways.

For many in the African American community, a lack of educational opportunities inside or outside of prison and a dearth of jobs in poverty-stricken neighborhoods has created a virtual 'revolving door' to prison.

Easy prey — pot smokers

Marijuana (cannabis) has been and remains the most popular prohibited drug in America. An estimated 71 million Americans have tried it at least once, including President Bill Clinton, Vice President Al Gore, House Speaker Newt Gingrich, and many other lawmakers and officials. An estimated eleven million Americans from all walks of life consume it regularly. About half of all college students have tried it. Its social prevalence, casual use, and the absence of violence associated with it make those who possess and consume 'pot' easy prey.

Since 1965 there have been over eleven million people arrested for marijuana. In 1996, alone, there were 641,642 marijuana arrests. The FBI reported that about 42 percent of all drug arrests that year were for pot, and that 85 percent of those were for simple possession. This means only fifteen percent of these arrests were for growing ('manufacture'), sale, or importation. About 37,000 marijuana offenders are behind bars today.

Some argue that the Drug War is financed by cannabis prohibition, because if we legalize that herb, there will not be much illegal drug use left to combat. Certainly, the two million or so consumers of other illicit drugs are not enough to rationalize spending some $16 billion of our taxes each year on federal drug prohibition. This does not even include the vast amounts of money spent by state and local governments to arrest, prosecute, and incarcerate marijuana offenders, or the parole violators who face a life sentence over a third strike offense for pot possession.

Special interests and profiteering

Building and running prisons for profit is a trend that demands a growing prison population to increase revenues, and turning more people into prisoners creates a need for more prisons. It's no coincidence that the two biggest campaign contributors in California in recent years have been the Police Officers Association and the Prison Guards union.

Lee with his wife and daughter, Yvonne.

Lee Augarten

age 40, serving 20 years

charged with conspiracy to distribute marijuana

The way it works is simple. Special interests who profit from the Drug War donate money to the campaigns of politicians who criminalize more social activities and send more people to prison for longer times. The prison industry pockets the profit, then recycles it back to pay off their political allies for the next round.

Investment reports of companies that sell to prisons, such as Joy Food Service, glowingly report to their stockholders that "Sales are just about doubling every year."

"The war on drugs is a failure and a success. It's a failure in that it has not stopped drug use in the country; a miserable failure," said Jack Crowley, former warden of Granite State Prison, Oklahoma. "But it's a great success because it's the best economic boom we have ever seen. It's provided jobs for people like me, for policemen, lawyers, judges, people that make guns and belly chains, people that run prisons; now the private prison industry. It's a boom!"

Private prisons

Now you, too, can earn dividends by owning stock in one of the fastest growing industries in America — private prisons. There are now seventeen companies in the private prison industry, holding some 80,000 prisoners in about 100 facilities in twenty states. Business is expected to double in five years.

With about 75 percent of the market worldwide, Corrections Corporation of America (CCA) and Wackenhut Corrections Corporation, are two of the biggest companies in the business of warehousing human beings. Forbes Magazine listed Wackenhut Corrections among the '200 Best Small Companies in America' in terms of profits. In its annual report, Wackenhut claims that, "Based on the 1.7 million people presently incarcerated in federal, state and local institutions and the historical rate of growth of approximately eight percent, there is a need to build more than 100,000 prison beds every year in the foreseeable future. We anticipate that the privatized corrections industry will be providing twenty percent of the new expansion beds each year."

Profits flow from contracts for 'revenue-producing beds.' Wackenhut boasts that sev-eral new contracts, awards for new state facilities, and a federal contract with the BOP make it "the largest provider of correctional services to the US federal government."

Claiming to provide these services cheaper than the government, the private prison industry lobby has increasingly influenced politicians looking to ease prison overcrowding while saving money.

However, a recent GAO report shows that private prisons do not save money. Further, receiving a per diem per inmate regardless of actual costs, companies' profit motives works against the prisoners' interests. Efforts to 'cut corners' by staffing fewer positions, spending less time training guards, and skimping on inmates activities may increase profits, but make prisons more dangerous. With less government oversight, reports of beatings and mistreatment are coming to light, as well as punitive measures being taken against prisoners to hold inmates as long as possible, to ensure that these 'revenue-producing' beds are filled.

Towns hard hit by economic downturns are reduced to competing with each other for private prisons. Looking for a new source of tax money, a source of jobs for its residents, and a way to spur development and attract businesses, towns offer free land, cheap utilities, and other incentives to lure prisons to their communities. A $79 million private prison has brought new development, new housing, a motel, a McDonald's restaurant and new tax revenue to a town in Missouri. Florida officials have a color brochure to promote prison economics and states, "a prison with 1,158 beds is worth $25 million a year and 350 jobs to a community." Openings include prison guards, counselors, teachers and managers.

Private prisons provide jobs and make high profits for a few people. On the other hand, how much will they ultimately cost the American system of justice by destroying more human lives in order to operate more prisons?

Founded in 1983 by investors behind Kentucky Fried Chicken, Corrections Corporation of America has been ranked among the top five performing companies on the New York Stock Exchange over the past three years.
Its value has risen from $50 million in 1986 to $3.5 billion in 1997.
— *The Nation* magazine, Jan. 5, 1998

David Ciglar

**age 39, serving 10 years
charged with
marijuana cultivation**

David with wife, Laurie, and their children.

*A hero who saved more
than 100 lives*

Before his arrest in Oakland, California, David Ciglar was being retrained for a promising new career as an MRI technician.

He had been injured on his job as a firefighter/paramedic as he was carrying a woman from a building. He has been credited with saving over 100 lives. Based on a tip to the DEA, he was caught with a plastic tray of 167 small marijuana seedlings growing in his garage.

Under a threat that his wife would also be sent to prison and his children sent to a foster home, David pleaded guilty. His family home was seized. He received the mandatory minimum sentence of ten years.

Is the community really safer for having lost a hero like David Ciglar behind bars for a decade?

"My family is devastated. My wife is living every day wondering if she can make it financially and mentally.

"My kids don't know why their dad was taken away for such a long, long time. I have not even bonded with my youngest daughter. She was just two when I left her.

"It will be proven in the near future that this is a miracle plant and the federal government has destroyed my life over it."

Gregory Kinder

age 42, serving 10 years
charged with possession
of 21 grams of LSD

Prison labor:
Factories behind fences

Paying slave wages for forced labor; knowingly employing illegal aliens; violating federal labor laws; failure to pay federal and state taxes; failure to pay workman's compensation and Social Security tax; operating a business without proper licenses and permits: The basis for a criminal indictment? No, just business as usual at UNICOR, a $500 million-per-year corporation under the federal Department of Justice.

Now you don't need to look to other countries like China to criticize prison labor. We have it right here in America, competing for your job. Setting long sentences for non-violent drug offenders keeps the number of prisoners up and creates a more stable, experienced, and easily controlled prison labor force.

Created in 1930 by an act of Congress to combat 'inmate idleness' and 'train prisoners in marketable work skills,' Federal Prison Industries (aka UNICOR) currently operates over eighty factories in 48 federal prisons around the country. Employing from 18 to 25 percent of federal inmates, UNICOR produces a variety of products and services such as clothing, furniture, stainless steel counters, signs, electronic wiring, cables, data entry, etc. The products have a guaranteed market — federal agencies that are required to shop first at UNICOR, whether or not the goods are less expensive or better made.

Former POW Patricia Ann Carmichael,

age 40, noted, "We sit here warehoused to serve our time. The employment opportunities available in the Federal System are UNICOR, which is 'slave labor' and taking civilian jobs and giving them to inmates at slave wages." American manufacturers are also complaining that this policy cripples competition and public bidding for contracts, and that it is causing a rise in bankruptcies. Labor unions are concerned that their jobs are being undermined. After all, what private business and workers can compete against a company that pays an average of sixty cents per hour?

The average cost of labor in the private sector is $9 an hour. And non-UNICOR prison labor pays even less: starting around eleven to twelve cents per hour for inmate labor! All inmates, federal or state, who are physically and mentally able must work, for which they are paid a small wage. A portion goes to pay court-ordered fines, victim restitution, and other obligations. Inmates complain that UNICOR offers low-level vocational training for assembly-line type jobs working with outmoded equipment and production techniques that have little to do with outside employment. Further, they offer no job placement services upon release.

All fifty states have prison industries that contract or lease their work force to public agencies or private businesses. According to a Jim Hightower report, inmates have made jeans and toys for JC Penney and Eddie Bauer in Tennessee, car parts for Honda in Ohio, uniforms for McDonald's in Oregon, and taken reservations for TWA. Oklahoma State Industries stated that "companies are attracted to working with prisons because inmates represent a readily available and dependable source of entry-level labor that is a cost-effective alternative to work forces found in Mexico, the Caribbean Basin, Southeast Asia,

> The UNICOR pay scale ranges from $0.23/hr to $1.15 /hr. (at increments up to an additional 30 cents per hour after seven years).

Mark Printz

age 33, served a 5 year sentence
charged with marijuana cultivation

"I have made a promise to myself that I will dedicate my time and resources to changing the laws here."

Mark with his family.

"I was diagnosed in 1991 with manic depressive illness, bi-polar disorder, and placed on Lithium as high as 2050 mg per day. This caused many side effects including tremors. I found that by smoking marijuana I was more relaxed and had no manic episodes.

"My self-treatment of marijuana as well as my desire to supply a few people who needed it for side effects of chemo for free in addition to the fact that I really enjoyed growing the plants as a form of therapy led to the waste of the last 3-1/2 years of my life.

"My parents and my children and perhaps my ex-wife, too, are being punished more than myself by me being incarcerated. We know of a friend of ours who was convicted of DUI manslaughter while using alcohol and was given house arrest. I fail to see how this prison time has done anything more than to make myself and my family outraged at our current state of political affairs.

"It seems that most of the people in prison are here for non-violent crimes. It is sad that this country which is supposed to be about freedom locks up so many of its citizens for medicating themselves with pot instead of alcohol.

"I have been in medium and low security prisons and there was always plenty of drugs and alcohol available. I have also been to two minimum facilities and there is still whatever you want. ... Despite what the BOP says, most contraband is brought in by staff and not from visits. This includes 'soft' contraband like small TV's, CD players and cell phones as well as 'hard contraband.' BOP personnel are on the bottom end of the pay scale and society and besides making a buck by smuggling for inmates they steal food and other supplies from the prison itself. Oh well... Only in America...

"I have made a promise to myself that I will dedicate my time and resources to changing the laws here. I hope to be able to do this work from inside the states but with the way things are headed in this country it might be time to get out while we still can. Kind of sounds like Germany before W.W.II."

and the Pacific Rim countries. 'Domestic content is an important benefit of using a prison-based work force compared with using an offshore labor market," says one industry executive. He went on to say, 'We can put a Made-in-the-USA label on our product.'"

Prison conditions — In the belly of the beast

Prison conditions vary from prison to prison, some are better and some are worse. Despite what some politicians would have us believe, none are 'country clubs.' With budget reductions a high priority, prisons and prisoners needs are the first to be cut. More and more prisons are eliminating education programs and Pell grants that previously have given the inmates opportunities to improve themselves before getting out, weight rooms that relieve tension and violence, and even drug treatment programs that help inmates break the cycle of addiction and recidivism. With uniform hair cuts being enforced in some prisons and many units in long-term lockdown, the trend is more towards dehumanizing inmates into hardened criminals than it is promoting rehabilitation.

Inmates and media alike acknowledge that rape is common in prison, and gangs operate within its walls. Women inmates in Georgia, California and elsewhere have been used as sex slaves, or sold as prostitutes by the guards. Drugs and disease proliferate. In California, officials admitted in October, 1997 that 41 percent of state inmates are infected

> "I would like to tell the public how many women I saw die or in the process of dying in prison [while in the medical facility].
>
> "Women who had no business in prison to begin with. Does the public really know their tax dollars are going to lock up tons of sick and elderly people, being kept alive on life support, so the feds can get every last breath out of them?
>
> "And who can justify keeping a 71 year-old woman, paralyzed from the neck down in prison?"
>
> **— Carol Cohn, Drug War POW**

with a potentially fatal virus, Hepatitis C. They offered no plan to address the problem. Tuberculosis and HIV infections are on the rise in prisons, too.

Though prison medical care is supposed to be held to the same standard as the private health care industry, many inmates report that their ailments are ignored and often left untreated until a crisis occurs. Some have been near death or accused of being on "hunger strikes" when they are suffering from ailments that do not allow them to eat. Medications and surgeries are often withheld.

A training video made for Brazoria County Detention Center, a private prison operating in Texas, shows guards kicking a crawling inmate in the groin and head and allowing a German shepherd dog to bite the man's leg. Other scenes included a deputy using a stun gun to shock inmates lying on the floor and a handler permitting a dog to bite several prisoners.

An incident that harkens back to the Roman empire and gladiator bouts has come to light in California. Seven inmates were shot to death by guards at Corcoran Prison in Kings County, and more than forty others have suffered gunshot wounds. Eight guards were indicted for staging fights among inmates in the prison exercise yard and then shooting at them. Attorney General Dan Lungren conducted a ten month investigation into violence at the prison, but filed no criminal charges. The Department of Corrections also failed to do so. But the FBI investigated, and guards were indicted "despite intentional efforts on the part of correctional and other officials to stymie, delay and obstruct our inquiry." Grand jury or FBI probes are among the tools needed to consider more charges at the highest levels of government.

What goes on behind prison walls, in the belly of the beast, needs to be investigated. After all, most inmates will eventually get out. How they are treated on the inside will reflect on how they behave on the outside which affects all of society.

Jodie Israel
age 34, serving 11 years
charged with marijuana conspiracy

"It is awful to see a human being caged like an animal."

"Since I have been in the system, we have had many women come in with four and six month sentences for taxes, etc. Armed bank robbers seem to be getting around five years, and the ones that are here for drugs are doing the lengthy sentences."

"I would like to express the great inhumanities I witnessed in transit with the US Marshals. Having been at a Federal Prison Camp-FPC, for ten months in Texas, I elected to move to a FPC in Dublin, California, closer to my family. On June 19, 1995, the marshals picked me and 6 other women up to transport us. We were black-boxed, leg shackled, and put into a van with heavy steel grating inside, and tinted windows, we were barely able to see out.

"We stopped at Fort Worth Medical Facility for male prisoners, and picked up a man. This man had no teeth in the front of his mouth at all, he had his hair braided at one time, and it had been so long since he had been able to take care of it, that the braids were matted together. As we drove on, he made conversation, telling us he had been in the hole for ninety days. The man seemed starved for human interaction. All eight of us were taken to Mansfield County Jail.

"After many hours of sitting in a holding tank, we were told we would be sleeping on the floor of the holding tank with a mattress. One woman had had a baby two weeks prior by Cesarean section, and it would have been very difficult for her. We were finally given a room, a vinyl mattress, and a wool blanket, no sheet or pillow, or sleeping clothes. From the window in our cell block, just two feet away, I watched a man in a steel, closed-in cell, with a food tray opening in the door, and a very small four by six inch window. What I saw I will never forget. The jail had a phone on wheels, they rolled up to the food tray slot, and he was able to make phone calls. As I watched him dialing and then hanging up before there was even time for a connection, I assumed he was just dialing for something to do. It was awful to see a human being caged like an animal.

"On June 20, we were again black-boxed, shackled, and driven on to Oklahoma City. On June 21, we were told to get our bedrolls ready, the marshal would be there soon for the airlift. The women were all put in a holding cell, thirty-some of us. An older woman with us told me that her husband was very ill, and they had left a halfway house, so they could spend what might have been their last days together. While we were in the holding tank, the men were marched by in groups to be processed. As I watched, an older man in the group walked by with a cane. His wife spotted him and they looked at each other and held their hands up at each other. It was heartbreaking to think that will probably be her last memory of him.

"After the men were processed we were taken out of the holding cell, five at a time to be strip searched, and then shackled and chained. After all the women were ready, we were taken to a long corridor, about 1/2 mile long. Along the right hand side of the corridor was prisoner after prisoner, all shackled and chained. Instead of feeling human, it felt more like we were cattle being shipped to the slaughter house, so dehumanizing. The sight of so many prisoners and of how their families will suffer and what they will have to endure made me ill. It was a sight I will never be able to get out of my mind."

What about the children?

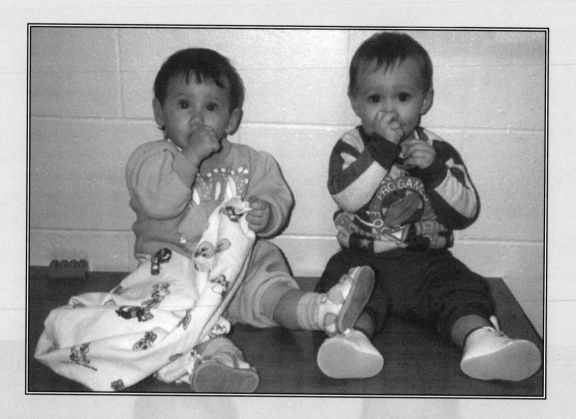

The twins spent their first birthday with their mom, Nancy Simmons, in the prison visiting room.

"No one is spared; no one is spared:
the sick, the elderly, children,
babies and pregnant women."

— Anne Frank describing the Nazi Holocaust

IV.
Hidden Body Count, Unseen Victims

The fact that women comprise the fastest growing population in prison today illustrates the broad net that has been cast in the Drug War.

From 1980 to 1994, the number of women in prison increased five-fold. Since federal mandatory minimum sentences were enacted in 1987, the number of women inmates has tripled. The majority of these women are first-time, nonviolent, low-level offenders. Yet, the plight of women prisoners gets very little media attention or political discussion. They have become the 'hidden body count.'

An increase in the number of female drug couriers, known as mules, is partly to blame for the gain in these statistics. Some women with children, facing difficult economic times, turn to drug trafficking activities to make ends meet. More often, however, the growing number of women in prison can be attributed directly to the inclusion of conspiracy convictions in the mandatory minimum sentencing scheme.

Charges of 'conspiracy' that prosecute all the defendants with every aspect of the alleged crime, no matter how minor the role they actually played, have rounded up many women. Keeping track of books, bank accounts or money, taking telephone calls, being a passenger in a car carrying drugs, or having their home used by someone else for drug dealing, despite their minimal involvement in such activities or even complete lack of knowledge are examples of the types of things that can land a woman in prison for ten years or longer.

Marcella with her son, Weston.

Marcella Robinson
age 32, sentenced to 10 years
charged with LSD conspiracy

In 1995, the combined incarceration rate for white and Latin-American women was 68 per 100,000. For African-American women, the rate was 456 per 100,000.
— Bureau of Justice Statistics, 1996

Bonnie Maki

age 47, serving 10 years

**charged with intent to manufacture
and distribute methamphetamine**

"I have made the greatest mistake of my life, but to take ten years of my life is wrong. If I could have stayed home, I would have spent the rest of my life proving to my community and friends and family that I was not the monster the law said I was. I have so much guilt in my heart for what I done to my children, because I was not strong enough to leave my husband when I wanted to. I will never forgive myself.

"I feel that it is not me that is being punished, but my children. I have three meals a day and clothes, and a roof over my head, and my children were left out there in the street by themselves. My son was thirteen and my daughter was fifteen when they took me away from them. I had never been away from them. Being in prison is so hard to describe because the pain you feel, the helplessness and the injustice tears you to pieces each day you face in here. I had never done anything illegal in my forty years on earth."

Many women in prison have a history of sexual or physical abuse prior to their incarceration. Some claim to be in abusive relationships that they've found it hard to extricate themselves from, realizing only in prison that they should have left when they had the chance. Like Kemba Smith, afraid to leave her man and ignorant of the drug conspiracy laws that hold all members equally culpable, they find out too late the price they must pay for their loyalty.

A poor choice of a boyfriend or being married to a man involved in drug activities has resulted in many wives and girlfriends being found guilty by association. Some, like Michelle Avery and Hamedah Ali Hasan, have been 'sacrificed' by the men in their lives, who implicated them in an offense in exchange for having their own sentences reduced.

Many women are being imprisoned for 'aiding and abetting' or 'misprision of a felony' simply for knowing about a situation and not reporting it to the police, or even for a situation authorities claim they *should* have known about. For refusing to 'cooperate' with law enforcement in convicting husbands and boyfriends, women are forced to pay the highest price of all — the loss of their freedom and their children.

For this reason, prisons are quickly filling up with women who's biggest offense is that they have little or no information to trade for a reduction of their sentences.

> **"Too often, women come into the prison system broken, betrayed by men, grieving over the loss of their role as caregiver to their children, estranged from parents, less educated than they want to be, traumatized by incest or sexual abuse, not knowing how to pull themselves back together."**
> **— *Guylan Gail Paul, 'Women's Spirituality in Prison,' Federal Prisons Journal, Spring 1992***

Kemba Smith

age 27, serving 24 years

charged with conspiracy to distribute crack cocaine, money laundering, false statements

Paying a terrible price for a poor choice.

Kemba with her son, William.

Kemba Smith was raised an only child of professional parents in a suburb of Richmond, Virginia. She considered her life sheltered and serene. Her parents made the decisions in her life, and imposed strict curfews and rules. She was not allowed to date until she was a senior at her predominantly 'white' high school.

When it came time for college, Kemba wanted to get the 'Black experience.' She chose Hampton University. There she met a popular guy, Peter Hall, who was well-known on campus but not a student. Kemba was impressed by his easy-going and self-confident manner, his Jamaican accent, nice clothes and fancy cars. He swept many women off their feet, and when he became interested in her, she felt like she found her 'knight in shining armor.'

It wasn't until later in their relationship that Kemba found out that Hall was considered to be a leader of one of the major drug distribution rings in the Mid-Atlantic region. As their relationship grew more intense, he exerted more and more control over her, and became both physically and verbally abusive.

When Hall was 'on the run,' Kemba dropped out of college and went with him. She was naive of the law and "always worried about him and never considered the trouble that I could get in."

When she was five months pregnant with his child, Hall convinced her to go home. Upon her return she learned that she was considered a 'fugitive,' and knew that she had to turn herself into the authorities. By the time Kemba was convinced that her only hope for her release would be to reveal the whereabouts of Hall, it was too late. He had been murdered in Seattle. Although the prosecutor admitted that she never actually handled or sold drugs, Kemba was held accountable for the entire amount of crack cocaine distributed by the conspirators, even though she had not known Hall when the conspiracy began.

Her baby was born in prison. She hopes to win her appeal to get 'a second chance' and help other young women avoid the mistakes she has made.

Kemba's cause has been taken up by students and journalists around the country as a prime example of excessive penalties for a low-level offender.

Jacquie Fogel

age 38, serving 10 years

charged with conspiracy to distribute marijuana, aiding and abetting

"I think Mandatory Minimums for first time offenders of non-violent crimes are criminal in themselves".

"Two years later, in 1988, I was arrested for my involvement in '85 and '86. I knew in my heart I had done nothing wrong other than being caught in something I could not foresee or control. I did the only thing possible, I left [quit the job]. The government said I should have reported what I saw regardless of the seemingly trivial nature. Because I didn't go to the police I was considered a part of the conspiracy.

"I damaged myself by my own statements when I was arrested. How was I to know that honesty is not the best policy? I answered all their questions to the best of my ability only to have them turn my words around to be used against me, i.e. I said 'I wasn't stupid I knew something was going on that wasn't right and I quit on the spot.' They said I said, 'I knew something was going on, I wasn't stupid.'

"The judge did not want to give me the Mandatory Minimum of ten years, but the DA was pushing hard for it, so he had no choice. I now know that justice is a scam, like so many other things in life. I know that accused people have very little hope in the court room. It is the jury who convicts us and the DA who sentences us. The judge does not have the power any longer to give just sentences based on the facts of the crime. It makes no difference except to myself that I am a model prisoner (if there is such a thing).

"A weaker person, one who doesn't have my optimistic viewpoint, would probably have a hard time making it with these draconian sentences, because we literally have

nothing to live for, except for a very distant future. Prison doesn't provide rehabilitation for those who made a mistake, it is a camp that breeds violence and discontent.

"I hope that I can remain close to the person that I was before this all began. I dream of being with my children before they become adults who no longer need me.

"I think Mandatory Minimums for first time offenders of non-violent crimes are criminal in themselves. I cannot believe that the government puts so little value on the lives of people and children.

"I have watched murderers and child molesters go home and come back, bank robbers leave and make the next heist and come back like it was nothing out of the ordinary. But let a first time non-violent drug related offender be given a mandatory minimum sentence, and they will stay here for ten years or more. If I had used a gun and killed someone, I would be home right now with my children.

"After being warehoused and allowed to vegetate while the rest of the world passes us by, we will be released. After spending so many years locked up, we are almost destined to fail because we will be so far behind the times. Then of course there is the stigma of being an ex-convict. They may as well given us a life sentence because the odds grow against us each year we're here without an education.'

"Taking the Pell Educational Grants is removing one of the most effective measures in stopping the revolving door of incarceration."

Children: The unseen victims

The Universal Declaration of Human Rights Article 16.3 states, "The family is the natural and fundamental group unit of society and is entitled to protection by society and the state."

Yet those who perhaps suffer most from Drug War policies are the children. They are the unseen victims — left behind to endure the traumatic separation from their parents when long prison sentences are imposed.

In a literal sense, they are being punished, too. When their parents are taken away, the children are sentenced to five, ten, twenty years without their parents love, nurturing, or support. The loss of a mother or father is extremely difficult for any child, under any circumstances. Psychologists have compared the loss of one's parents to the prison system to experiencing a death in the nuclear family. Parents and children grieve each other's absence, and miss them in their lives.

Many children are displaced from their schools and communities when their families are split apart. Brothers and sisters are often separated from each other and moved into different homes, as the burden of caring for more than one child is shared by the extended family or support network. So, in addition to losing their parents and homes, these siblings also often lose each other.

It is difficult for children to cope with all these significant losses in their lives, which

One Drug War POW's child wrote a note to her asking, "Mommy, if I be bad, can I come where you are?"

• **A majority of women in federal prison are there for drug law violations; 70% are first time offenders.**
• **Over 113,000 women are incarcerated in prisons and jails in the US.**
• **Over 75% of female prisoners and approximately 60% of male prisoners are parents.**
• **Over 40% of women prisoners were physically or sexually abused prior to prison.**

Sources: JusticeWorks Community. *Parents in Prison, Children in Crisis* Fact Sheet

---

may result in behavioral problems, failure in school, and overall dysfunction. They feel angry, lonely, abandoned, and alienated. Some feel ashamed and different from other kids. This can lead to very serious problems. A nationwide survey of troubled children in the juvenile justice system shows that prisoners' children are five times more likely to end up in prison than are other children. They may also harbor hostility or fear towards authority, whom they perceive as being responsible for their situation.

As Calvin Treiber writes, "My mom says my little girl is scared to death when she sees a cop riding down the street in their car cause she knows the cops took her mamma and daddy."

Deborah with her daughter, Heather.

Deborah Lynn Mendes

age 41, serving 12 years, 7 months
charged with conspiracy to aid and abet
in distribution of cocaine,
career criminal enterprise

"How very naive I was."

Deborah Mendes was enjoying a successful career as an assistant Vice President and branch manager for the Bank of America when she was offered a position by a former practicing attorney who had several commercial accounts at her bank. He represented a group of foreign investors who were involved in real estate and other business transactions in the US and overseas.

Her indictment alleged that she assisted these investors in drug trafficking activities by managing their funds, purchasing and leasing residences and commercial warehouses to store cocaine, and depositing drug proceeds in less than $10,000 increments to avoid Federal Currency Reporting requirements.

Although the prosecution called seventy witnesses at the trial, none of these witnesses provided first-hand testimony that she knowingly and willfully participated in a conspiracy to distribute cocaine. The case was based entirely on circumstantial evidence relating to her involvement in financial and real estate transactions on behalf of the investment company. She had no knowledge of the illegal activities of her employers.

In July 1992, she returned from Mexico where she was living and self-surrendered to the authorities, anxious to clear her name and prove herself innocent of the charges against her.

"Unfortunately, I thought I simply had to turn myself in, tell my story and 'Liberty and justice for all' would prevail. How very naive I was.

"I am not the only one to suffer. My parents are devastated. They feel guilty because they helped convince me that coming back from Mexico and turning myself in was the right thing to do. My sisters and their families have also been seriously affected by all of this. Most of all, my children are suffering. They lost their father to cancer, five years ago, their mother one year later [to the criminal justice system] and at the same time lost each other by having to live in separate homes, hundreds of miles apart."

Nancy Simmons

age 43, serving 10 years

charged with conspiracy to distribute cocaine

Letter from Nacole Simmons
Nancy's 14-year-old daughter

I want you to know that I miss you, Mom. Deep in my heart I am lonely without you. Even though I have my dad, at this time in my life I need a Mom. Ever since you've been gone I'm feeling so all alone without you.

I need your help, Mom. So many days have gone by and not one I haven't stopped and thinking of you. So many memories of your face I see every day.

Sometimes it feels like the world is on my shoulders and it starts to get heavier and heavier. Everywhere I go you are always in my heart.

    With love,
    Nacole

Nancy Simmons, top center, with her mother and children. Nacole is in the center of the group.

"I am serving this ten year sentence in a Minimum Security Prison. They call it a Prison Camp. I am such a danger to society that I am in a prison that has no fences, no bars, no prison cell. There are only one to two officers on the compound that are watching (baby-sitting) us. Some 300 to 325 women are here.

"Everyday when my children are spread apart from each other, someone is preparing their daily meal at dinner time. About 400 miles away, their mother is sitting on a bunk bed, listening to music, crocheting, reading, writing a letter, or just relaxing...something is terribly wrong with this picture. There are other alternatives to this situation, solutions that would benefit the welfare of the children."

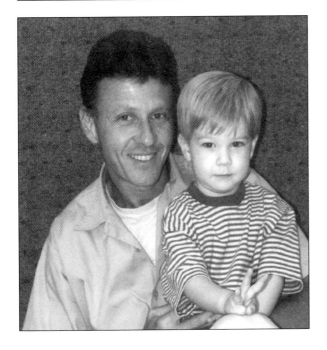

Martin Sax

age 49, serving 21.8 years

charged with conspiracy to distribute marijuana, money laundering

"My wife has been left to raise our son all by herself. She has no help and Benjamin has no father to put him to bed at night. My little boy will never know what it's like to have his Daddy tuck him in bed, give him a kiss, and read him a bedtime story....

"If the laws don't change, my little boy will be 20 years old before I get out."

Martin with his son, Benjamin

Laichem Sae Lee

age 34, serving 10 years

charged with conspiracy to import and distribute opium

"My children cry for me. I only talk to them on the phone and only through my imagination can I see them and through photographs that my family sends from home.

"I am thousands of miles away from my children.... I have seen my children once in four years.... They are not coping well with the loss of both their parents."

Laichem with her children, Nick, Nancy, Linda and Danny.

Vivienne Hopkins

age 35, serving 10 years

charged with possession with intent to distribute and import cocaine

"I didn't have income for almost three months. My ex-husband cut off the child support he was sending. This led me to seek help through social services. Someone approached me on how to make a little quick money. Said I couldn't get in any serious trouble since I had never been in any trouble before....

"I have made a mistake that I feel I have paid plenty for at the cost of my children... We all need to show people we are not serious criminals. Most of us didn't feel we had another choice to care for our families.

"All my years of staying out of trouble didn't count for anything. I gave ten years in the military reserves and it didn't count for anything either.

"How can it be justice to take a sole caregiver from her family and let the children suffer so much?"

Vivienne and her daughter, Destinee.

Parent/child relationship

Lacking alternatives to incarceration, the parent /child bond is hard to sustain at a distance. No matter how hard they try to maintain contact, it is extremely difficult and frustrating for parents in prison to 'parent' their children at such a distance. Through letters or expensive phone calls, they try to retain a role in their children's lives, but nothing can replace being there.

The removal of parents from their children's lives is even more complete when they are sent to prisons that are hundreds or thousands of miles away from their family homes. Travel costs are prohibitive for many families, which prevents them from visiting their loved ones in prison. For Laichem Sae Lee and her children, that means years between visits and physical contact with each other.

When children get someone to take them to visit a parent, the hours are limited, the environment of the visiting area is cold, confining and lacking in privacy, and the pain of leaving each other at the end of the day is emotionally draining. When taken from their families when their children are very young, parents often fear that their children may not know them when they get out of prison. David Ciglar's daughter was only two when he was arrested. She will be ten or eleven by the time he comes home. Only then will they begin to know each other. Missing such a vital period in a child's early development can never be replaced.

For some children, the separation from their mothers can be permanent. Mothers who are forced to give up maternal rights often have a difficult time reclaiming their own children upon release, especially if the child is not living with relatives or friends.

Sometimes mothers lose track of their children altogether in the foster care system as their children are shifted from family to family. Being dependent on prison officials, who may be indifferent to their children's needs or whereabouts, makes it especially difficult to find them.

Lovetta with her son, Stanley, and daughter, Kaniesha.

Lovetta Clark

age 43, serving 30 years

charged with conspiracy to import and distribute cocaine

"My children are the ones that are suffering the most. My son, Stanley, always asked me, 'Mama, when are you coming home?'

"I replied, 'soon.'

"After six years he said, 'Mama, soon sure takes a long, long time.'"

Mom
This is
what i'd
like to
do when
you get
out....

Army tank

Victor

Jail
Jail

I love
you
Mom ♡

The son of a Drug War POW made this card for his mother.

Born behind bars

Another circumstance to be considered is that of the many pregnant women who enter the criminal justice system and their children. In an article entitled "Care of the Pregnant Offender", Anita Huft, Lena Sue Fawkes, and W. Travis Lawson, Jr. wrote about this aspect in the Spring, 1992 Federal Prisons Journal.

"Women in Federal prisons do not directly care for their infants after birth. Developing a maternal role therefore depends upon plans for placing the infant after birth.

"The inmate can place the infant either for adoption or for guardianship. She may choose to maintain a maternal role 'in absentia' or relinquish her parental role to a relative or friend, depending on factors such as support systems in prison, the inmate's self-esteem, the presence of an intact family on the outside, and the imminence of release.

"In addition to losing freedom, privacy, and self-esteem, inmates must also cope with losing a child and an identity as a mother."

The trauma of a police raid

It is traumatic for children to experience a police raid on their home. How does it affect children to see narcotics police or DEA agents break down their front door of their homes late at night or early in the morning, smashing windows, tearing the house apart? Too often, children watch in horror as agents throw their parents to the floor and aim guns at their heads. The children themselves are often held at gunpoint for hours. What happens to children who see police take the family car and home, and send their parents to prison for decades at a time?

It is ironic that a Congress with a governing ideology that prides itself on moralizing and claims to support 'family values' has failed so miserably in the area of providing alternative policies that strengthen families rather than destroy them. Perhaps it is time for our national leaders to take their own rhetoric seriously and move to reduce the harm that is routinely done to our families by the prisons and drug penalties.

• 1.5 million children have a parent in jail or prison; another 3.5 million children have a parent on parole or probation.

• Two out of three incarcerated women in the US have children under the age of eighteen.

• Eight to ten percent of women are pregnant when they enter prison; another 15% have babies less than six weeks old.

• It costs taxpayers $20,000 a year per child for foster care.

Sources: 1996 Prison Law Project of the National Lawyers Guild. Bureau of Justice statistics, 1995. JusticeWorks.

Carol Cohn

age 37, serving 5 years

**charged with possession of marijuana
with intent to distribute**

Carol's children had just gotten home from school when the police raided. Back to front: Dusty, Jake, Matt, Cruz.

"I went to jail three months pregnant. The jail I was in, the doctor told me not to eat the food or drink anything made with the water, as it came straight out of the Rio Grande, was contaminated and caused birth defects. Our cells were filled with roaches, rats and mice.

"While I was in jail for the first five days, the Texas feds called my local DEA and sheriff in Iowa and told them to raid my house. They couldn't have done it while the kids were at school. They waited until 4 pm; my kids get home at 3:50. My children were there with the babysitter at the time. My eleven-year-old (then nine) was out riding his bike, he was pulled over by the cops, told to park his bike and get in the squad car. He was told I was in jail, that I was under a million dollars bond, and that I was never getting out.

"They drove to my house and were met by other cops. My oldest, then fourteen, and his girlfriend were walking out the door. The cops proceeded to pull guns on them.

"They raided my house, did a lot of damage to my car and home on purpose. My oldest watched them search his room and drop something in his fish tank, he still doesn't know what. By evening, all the fish were dead.

"The agents dumped out my cabinet in the living room. When they finished, my son picked up all the stuff off the floor. One cop said, 'I didn't tell you to pick up nothing.' Then knocked the stuff out of his hands."

Diana Nelson

age 41, serving 30 years;

charged with conspiracy to possess with intent to distribute crack cocaine, aiding & abetting

Diana Nelson poses with her diploma. Her release date is October 14, 2015

How it happened

By Crystal Nelson

When I was 9 years old, my family was split apart when both my parents and three of my brothers were taken to prison for drugs. My parents always made sure their children had what they needed. My parents and brothers have been in prison for 6 years. It's hard for kids to 'be on their own.' The day they were taken to prison, I felt like my heart had jumped out of my chest and onto the ground, I hurt so bad.

When I was 15 years old, I had a summer job. I sent my parents money to help with their personal needs while in prison. My Mom makes 12¢ per hour, and my Dad $50 a month. Whenever I scrape up enough money to send to them, I do it. God has made a special place in my heart for children like me, because I know how it feels not to have your parents, or even one of them, to take care of you. My mom used to tuck her 4 kids in bed at night, and one night after she had tucked us all in, the police came jumping through our windows, breaking down doors, and worst of all, pointing guns at everyone in the house. Now that I know God is always there, I pray to Him every day to help me through the hardships in my life, and also to help my family through any problems they may have.

I also attend church whenever I go see my grandparents, about every other weekend. Because I am in a Girls' Home, I don't have any control over when I get to go to their house. But when I do go, I take my 6-year-old cousin, 3-year-old cousin, and 6-month-old nephew to church, because I feel they should know about God before their life starts getting harder. I learned the hard way, but I still thank God for keeping my family in contact.

I realize you have to be really strong to live this way.

Right: Top row, her sons Colin and Corey. Middle, her daughters Celeste and Crystal. Bottom row, her nephews Justin and Randy, and grandson C.J.

"We started selling drugs just to survive and live, and on Feb. 7, 1989, the police came and busted our house — knocked out windows, kicked in doors, held guns to my small children's heads — told them if they moved they would fire. They had to hold their arms out the side of their bed. This was 10:00 at night. There were three raids, in all of them they kicked out windows, an air conditioner fell in on my 1-year-old grandson; they took him to the hospital.

"My family was torn apart, my children were devastated. They have had a lot of hardship and problems since I've been locked up. They have been placed from home to home and here and there since I've been here. My parents kept them for 2-1/2 years after I got locked up, but it got to be too much for them, cause the children were angry and acted accordingly. One is now in a group home due to her anger and outbursts of rage.

"My family is still going through trials and the kids aren't really accepted because they come from a mixed marriage and have had to endure rough terrain."

Victor Plescia

age 53, serving 35 years

charged with delivery of cocaine,
use of a telephone to commit a felony

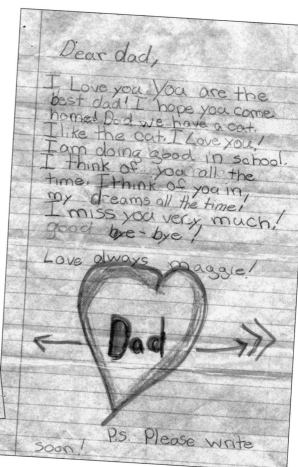

Dear dad,

I Love you. You are the best dad! I hope you come home! Dad we have a cat. I like the cat. I Love you! I am doing good in school. I think of you all the time. I think of you in my dreams all the time! I miss you very much! good bye-bye!

Love always, maggie!

← Dad →

P.S. Please write soon!

Daddy I Love you. you are the Best one. Dad I miss you dad. I hope you come home. I miss you. I Love you. come home. P.S. I miss

Victor's children, Ashley, Maggie, and Vic, Jr.

kleptocracy (klep-tó-crisi) *n. government by thievery*

—

"Civil asset forfeiture laws are being used in terribly unjust ways, depriving innocent citizens of their property with nothing that can be called due process. … You never have to be convicted of any crime to lose your property. You never have to be charged with any crime. In fact, even if you are acquitted by a jury on criminal charges, your property can be seized."
— *U.S. Rep. Henry Hyde (R, IL)*

"A law designed to give cops the right to confiscate and keep the luxury possessions of major drug dealers mostly ensnares the modest homes, cars and hard-earned cash of ordinary law-abiding people.

"This was not the way it was supposed to work."
— *U.S. Rep. John Conyers (D, MI)*

V.

Search and Seizure Fever

First they come with battering rams and guns to kick in the front door. Later they come back with legal documents and seize the house. Armed with a search warrant, drug agents rifle through your most personal of possessions, and cart away financial documents, diaries and everything of value.

The family car, the computer, valuables, all your cash, your bank accounts and investments, the business you built with your own hands, even your kid's piggy bank — all suddenly gone. Often you are left with no money to hire the necessary legal representation to defend yourself.

The Universal Declaration of Human Rights Article 17.2 states, "No one shall be arbitrarily deprived of his property." The US Constitution Fifth Amendment says no American shall be "deprived of life, liberty, or property, without due process of law". Chalk these up as two more victims of the Drug War.

The corrupting influence of unbridled greed has led to many personal tragedies. It doesn't matter whether or not you have any drugs. In fact, you can be acquitted of all charges and still lose everything. Federal and many state forfeiture laws empower governments to take people's private property without due process.

What is Civil Asset Forfeiture?

Civil Asset Forfeiture laws allow the government to seize property without charging anyone with a crime, and then keep it without ever having to prove a case. In forfeiture law, it is the property that is accused of a crime, not the owner. Lawyers call that *in rem* —

Latin for 'against the thing.' One odd result is case names such as 'US vs. $2, 452' or 'US vs. A Parcel of Land Known as 4492 South Lavonia Road.'

Beyond the Drug War and following in its wake, over 200 federal forfeiture laws have now been attached to non-drug offenses.

Seized property is presumed guilty and may be forfeited based upon mere hearsay, or even a tip supplied by an informant who stands to gain up to 25 percent of the forfeited assets. Since police get to keep nearly all the proceeds from forfeited property, there is an inherent conflict of interest. Officers often succumb to greed, budget pressures and the temptation of bounty in the form of seized assets for their departments. The Kubinskis are an example of a family who were not even left with enough of their own money to pay for lawyers.

Between 1985 and 1995, the federal Departments of Justice and Treasury seized more than $4 billion from US citizens, many of whom have not been charged with a crime. In fiscal year 1994 alone, federal forfeitures totalled $730,000,000.00.

In federal forfeiture cases, law enforcement gets to keep the seized assets. Some states provide that a portion goes into their General Fund. What property can the government take? Any property can be seized if the police suggest that it was:

• Bought from the profits of illegal activity.

• Used to facilitate a crime (such as a family car that was driven to buy drugs).

How much evidence does the government need for this? No hard evidence; just probable cause — the same standard required for a

Scott with his wife, Dawn, and children, Taylor and Michael.

Scott Walt

age 39, serving 24 1/2 years

charged with conspiracy to possess marijuana with intent to distribute

"[The agent] stated to me, 'We want to search your house. If we have to get a warrant we will bust your doors down, put guns to your wife and children's heads and tear your f____ house apart, or you can sign this waiver and we'll be nice.' Well, I signed the waiver. ... They found no drugs, no scales, no ledgers, nothing! They took financial records, a cell phone, our home phone and address book, and $7,350 in our bedroom. My wife was a team leader for Mary Kay Cosmetics and her office was in our home. She asked, 'Why are you taking the money.' They said, 'drug proceeds.' We shook our heads in disbelief. ...

"At sentencing the government wanted a fine of $250,000. ... The judge said, 'No fine; enough is enough. This man is getting far too much time, murderers receive less. If it weren't for the book, (he held up the sentencing guidelines), I would not be sentencing him to this. We'll all be dead and his marriage will be over.

"Enough is enough!'"

search warrant or arrest. Police can use hearsay evidence, such as a tip from an informant whose name is not revealed. In all other type of cases, hearsay is inadmissible.

Can seized property be reclaimed?

You must file a 'claim' that you are the owner of the seized property and, except for real estate or property worth more than $500,000, post a cash bond equivalent to ten percent of the value of the property in order to have the right to a hearing to contest the seizure.

At trial, the burden of proof is on you, not the government. You are required to prove that your property is innocent by a 'preponderance of the evidence' — a higher standard than the 'probable cause' standard used by police to seize the property.

If a person is found innocent in the criminal case, the government can still forfeit the property by filing a separate civil forfeiture case. Sounds like double jeopardy, but the Supreme Court said in 1996 that double jeopardy doesn't apply to civil forfeiture. That same year, the Court ruled that a completely innocent property owner can lose their property if it was used illegally by someone else.

Innocence is irrelevant!

Privacy: Your home is your castle

Privacy has long been held to be an implied right of the US Constitution, but just what this covers is vague and has been dramatically eroded over the course of the Drug War.

The Fourth Amendment protects us from "unreasonable searches and seizures", requiring that "no Warrants shall issue, but upon probable cause supported by Oath or affirmation, and particularly describing the place to be searched, and the persons or things to be seized."

Article 12 of the United Nations Universal Declaration of Human Rights states that, "No one shall be subjected to arbitrary interference with his privacy, family, home or correspondence, nor to attacks upon his honor and reputation. Everyone has the right to the protection of the law against such interference or attacks."

How does the government protect our privacy? Undercover agents pose as friends, police rifle through garbage, subpoena telephone and electrical bills, spy over fences, fly over homes, scan Americans with infrared sensors, heat detectors, x-rays and even use enhanced satellite surveillance photography to see what people are doing in their own homes and backyards.

Courts have ruled that forced chemical assay of hair and body fluids, phone taps and body cavity searches by police are not unreasonable to enforce laws against substances that have been prohibited.

'Big brother' has become a vivid reality.

Alfreda's Story

Alfreda Robinson

age 43, serving 10 years

charged with conspiracy to distribute crack cocaine

An educator with two masters degrees, Alfreda, considered herself a law abiding citizen. She was working as a high school counselor following seven years of teaching for the Baltimore City Public Schools. Up until her arrest and incarceration on conspiracy charges, the most 'serious' trouble she had been in amounted to driving on a suspended license for which she received probation from the DMV.

Alfreda was a single mother of an only son, David, a troubled youth who began selling drugs. Alfreda made it known to him that she was against this activity and made repeated efforts to rehabilitate him throughout his life. Twice she tried 'tough love' and put him out of her house when he was age sixteen and again at age eight-

een. She never stopped loving him, though, and assisted him when he needed help getting an apartment or buying used cars which were affordable on her salary.

When David was arrested, he called his mom from jail and asked her for help, once again. He needed money for an attorney, and a friend owed him some. He asked her to phone his friend's mother to get $4500. By placing this call, she became a 'conspirator' in his case. The morning of the raid, the $4500 in marked monies was found in her basement safe, placed there by David without her knowledge. Despite a complete lack of evidence placing Alfreda near any drug activity, the government used these monies to support the seizure of her house which was legally purchased with documented and verified funds from an automobile settlement.

Her son's friend turned informant and was given immunity for his testimony that resulted in a 45-year sentence for David and ten for Alfreda.

"Nothing prepared me for the education I am now receiving in prison. What did I do to deserve this, beside give birth to and love my child? I realize my son should not have been involved in illegal activities, but how do you put a 21-year-old in prison for 45 years, who sold drugs and never killed anyone, while a murderer serves an average of seven to fifteen years and returns to society? What is the message my son receives?"

Kenny surrounded by his children, Adam, Ariel and Katie.

After their family home was seized by the government, Adam Kubinski drew this picture and asked, "Mommy, is there a hole where my house was?"

Kenny Kubinski

serving Natural Life

charged with conspiracy to distribute marijuana, hashish, and cocaine, money laundering

Before their arrest, the Kubinskis were active members of their farm community.

Kenny cut and delivered firewood to elderly neighbors, volunteered his landscaping skills to Habitat for Humanity through the church, and provided jobs through his family construction company. Jackie was an active member at her church, a volunteer at her children's school, and a local board member for the American Diabetes Association.

Due to asset forfeiture, the Kubinskis have lost everything: their home, their business, their freedom and — at least for now — each other.

Following a traumatic separation, the children are learning to cope. They are able to visit Jackie once a month for a few hours at a time. They can only visit their father every three or four months, due to the long distance to the prison.

Jackie wrote, "They always ask, 'When are you coming home?'."

Jackie Kubinski

serving 6 1/2 years

charged with conspiracy to distribute marijuana, hashish, cocaine

"Mommy, is there a hole where my house was?"

Jackie Kubinski holds her children, Ariel, Katie and Adam.

Open letter from Jackie Kubinski

"On January 15, 1993, a Government Drug Task Force came to our house at 7:00 am and said the government was seizing all our property, personal and corporate. The American dream was snatched away from us, and this was only the beginning of a nightmare that still continues.

"No drugs were found and no arrests were made at the time the property was seized. The government alleged that my husband acquired his business with drug proceeds and has used the business to launder money....

"On April 30, 1993, we were arrested. The government did everything they could to prevent us from hiring a lawyer. My husband and his two brothers continued working their construction company, but when the company made money to pay bills, the money would be seized by the IRS from the corporation account.

"Our family had to sell all the company's equipment and ask both families for money to hire an attorney. We are presently destitute.

"I was charged with misprision of a felony* and money laundering. Then a few months later they added a superseding indictment charge and dropped the money laundering charge and added conspiracy to distribute cocaine, hashish, and marijuana. (At trial, 'misprision' was dropped and I was then charged with one count of conspiracy to distribute....)

"I began serving my sentence on November 15, 1993. Our children were put in an orphanage until friends from our church asked for custody to raise them in their home. I am presently in a prison for women in Butner, North Carolina.

"Our son Adam would get so mad, because he couldn't do anything to help get his mom and dad out of jail. On Thanksgiving day, he cried, 'I just want my own mom and dad and my own turkey and my own table.'"

---

* The offense of concealing knowledge of a felony by someone who has not participated or assisted in it.

Clyde Young, Sr.

**serving 26 years
charged with
marijuana conspiracy**

Police seized all their money, including piggy banks and an SSI check, as being drug profits, then took the family home.

Clyde Young, Sr. (center) with his family.

Clyde and Patricia Young were living with their eight children on the border of Mississippi and Alabama on land surrounded by the property of a wealthy businessman, J.P. Altmire.

In 1988, Altmire wanted to purchase their land. When they refused to sell, he wrote letters to lawyers, prosecutors, and the local sheriff branding the family a bunch of 'troublemakers.'

The Youngs refused to budge and in August of 1988, their eldest son was arrested for cultivating marijuana on Altmire's property. Their house was torn up with pick shovels and dogs. The police seized all the money in the house, including the children's piggy banks and a 90-year-old uncle's social security check. No drugs were found.

The following year, the house was raided again and the whole family was arrested, including the old uncle, Clyde's mother, sisters and brothers. At the indictment, the Youngs learned that 'drug residue,' a scale, and a notebook containing first names and references to amounts were found in a 1986 raid at the hunt club owned by Clyde's mother.

The trial judge was Altmire's former lawyer and friend, Charles Butler. Butler refused to allow the defense to admit the 36 letters Altmire sent to local authorities.

Prosecution witnesses included the police chief's grandson who was facing a long prison sentence for three prior drug convictions, a witness facing forty years for drug trafficking, and one who is now serv-

Patricia Young

serving 24 years, 8 months

charged with marijuana conspiracy

Clyde Young, Jr.

serving 15 years

charged with marijuana conspiracy

Above left: Patricia Young.

Above right: Clyde Young, Jr., surrounded by his family.

ing a seven-year sentence for perjury. Experts testified that the handwriting in the seized notebooks was not that of Patricia Young.

Clyde and Patricia Young and four of their children were found guilty of possession and conspiracy to distribute marijuana in an on-going criminal enterprise. Clyde was given 26 years. Patricia got 24 years, eight months. Their four children received fifteen, ten, five, and three years each.

Rest in Peace

Esequiel Hernandez
Bruce Lavoie
Scott Bryant
Rev. Accelyne Williams
John Fellin
Annie Rae Dixon
Shirley Dorsey
Manuel Ramirez
Donald Scott
Gary Shepherd
Robert Lee Peters
Gerardo Anthony Mosquera, Jr.
Chad MacDonald
Barbara & Kenny Jenks

Other fatalities

VI.
In Memorium

The foremost human right is the right to life, from which spring all other rights. In the words of the Universal Declaration of Human Rights Article 1, "Everyone has the right to life, liberty and the security of person."

This chapter is dedicated to those people caught in the cross-fire of turf wars due to the profit motive raised by illegal drugs; to those who died enforcing this counterproductive drug prohibition; to those who have been killed or injured in the 'friendly fire' of police raids or in raids based on bad tips or wrong addresses.

It is dedicated to those who suffer pain or death while denied access to medicine; to those who must defy the laws to obtain relief; to those who have contracted AIDS/HIV due to the Drug War mentality that has banned needle exchange programs; to those who have died from contaminated or misrepresented drugs as a result of the criminal market.

Finally, it is dedicated to all who have fought for the return of tolerance and justice, but who did not live to see that day come.

Why so many deaths and so much brutality, we may ask, particularly over such small quantities or even non-existent drug supplies? Part of the problem is a government policy of using excessive force and no-knock raids in their zeal to capture evidence and round up drug suspects. These are dangerous, high-risk tactics, using heavily armed masked men, entering homes unannounced at all hours without regard or even full knowledge of who is in the household, threatening families. Sometimes accidents happen.

When people get hurt or killed, no one is held responsible. No apologies are issued to the victim's family. But many if not most of these situations could have been avoided.

Each human life is precious, and when this kind of policy is allowed to endure, it diminishes our own humanity. So we must pause to reflect on the consequences and implications of these acts. We remember these civilian fatalities.

❧ Rev. Accelyne Williams

Boston police, acting on a tip by an informant, conducted a surprise no-knock raid on a city home. Retired Methodist minister Accelyne Williams was chased around his Massachusetts apartment by members of a police team looking for drugs and guns, when he collapsed and died of a heart attack at the age of 75.

No guns or drugs were found, as it was soon discovered they raided the wrong apartment.

❧ Bruce Lavoie

On August 3, 1989, Bruce Lavoie lay peacefully sleeping in the room he shared with his young son in the village of Hudson, New Hampshire. At five in the morning he was awakened by a loud noise as his whole home was shaken violently. A battering ram had smashed his front door, and a dark band of armed men rushed into his small apartment. Rising to defend his son, Lavoie was shot to death as his little boy watched helplessly.

Police found one marijuana cigarette butt.

> **a·troc'·i·ty (ă-tros'-i-ti) n. [from L. atrox, atrocis, meaning cruel] 1. enormous wickedness, extreme cruelty. 2. a specific act of brutality or cruelty.**

❧ Annie Rae Dixon

Age 84 and bedridden, Annie Rae Dixon was killed by police in a 1992 drug raid in East Texas. No drugs were found in her home. A 28-year-old officer said his automatic pistol accidentally discharged when he kicked open Mrs. Dixon's bedroom door.

Earlier that night, an informant was given $30 to go into the Dixon home, where he claimed he could buy some drugs. He later emerged with crack cocaine, but police did not search him either before or after the purchase.

The informant reported that a few young women and children lived there, but he didn't know about the sick woman. Police got a search warrant and returned to the house just after two o'clock in the morning. They sprinted up the ramshackle porch and smashed the front door with a battering ram. As they swept in, the officer kicked in the door to Ms. Dixon's bedroom and fell, slamming his elbow against the door and firing the gun. The officer said he collapsed and "started throwing my guts up crying because I knew I had shot somebody that didn't have no reason to be shot."

A memorial was set up at the spot where Esequiel Hernandez was killed by US Marines on a drug interdiction mission. Photo by James Evans.

❧ Robert Lee Peters

Deputies did not identify themselves before breaking into the St. Petersburg, FL, house as the family prepared to watch a video movie.

Age 33 at his time of death in July, 1994, friends and relatives say Robert L. Peters may have mistaken the police for burglars. Deputies did not know there were two children and his ailing stepfather (who had a heart attack after the shoot-out) in the house at the time of the no-knock raid. The police tried to smash through the front door with a battering ram. Peters fired a .357 magnum through the door and was struck three times by the SWAT team's return fire.

Two pounds of cannabis were seized from his home, and records indicate that a secret informer bought 7.3 grams of marijuana. An undercover detective purchased 27 grams. His brother George was charged and did not resist arrest.

George said his brother wouldn't have resisted either, had he known they were deputies. "All they had to do," he said, "was knock on the door."

❧ John Fellin

John Fellin was 34 years old when he was shot five times and killed by a special drug task force in his home on February 28, 1992 in West Hazleton, PA. He died in front of his live-in girlfriend and one of his three children, two-year old Vanessa.

Fellin had been arrested on charges of marijuana distribution in 1984. He had not been in trouble since.

Although the police claim that the 5'6", 140 pound Fellin attacked the 6'6" 260 pound police officer and was wrestling with him over the officer's shotgun, the family reported that the police never announced themselves and "entered the residence with a patently invalid search warrant" (based on two $10 marijuana buys from Fellin to an undercover police officer in July, 1991). One pound of marijuana, a triple-beam scale and some baggies were found.

His family called his untimely death "cold-blooded murder."

🌹 Esequiel Hernandez

May 14, 1979 – May 20, 1997

The first US citizen killed by military troops on US soil since 1970, when students were killed by National Guard troops at a Kent State University Vietnam War protest.

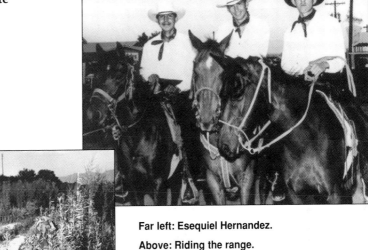

Far left: Esequiel Hernandez.

Above: Riding the range.

Left: A heavily armed soldier hides in the bushes, camouflaged in a 'ghillie suit.' Photo by James Evans.

Esequiel 'Zeke' Hernandez, born and raised in Texas, was considered one of Redford's "best and the brightest" with aspirations of becoming a game warden or park ranger. He was only eighteen years old at the time of his death, in the isolated border town of Redford, Texas (with a population of almost 100).

Esequiel was born the year before Ronald Reagan was elected President. Prior to Reagan's administration, the Posse Comitatus Act had prevented active duty military troops from engaging in domestic law enforcement. During his term it was amended to allow troops to be on patrol in the Drug War at home.

Zeke was tending his family goat herd when he was shot by 22-year-old Marine Corporal Banuelos, who was part of the Joint Task Force Six, a military unit assigned to anti-drug operations. The Marines, dressed in camouflage battle fatigues, were hiding in the bushes looking for drug smugglers.

While tending the goats, Zeke carried a rifle that his grandfather had given him to use to protect the goats from snakes and wild animals. The marines claim that he fired two shots in their direction, and upon seeing him raise his rifle again, Banuelos fired the fatal shot from an M-16. Townspeople claim they only heard one shot. The autopsy showed that Esequiel was not facing Banuelos when he was killed. He lay bleeding on the ground unattended for twenty minutes before he died.

The townspeople had no idea that Marines were patrolling the area in camouflaged outfits known as 'ghillie suits,' which make them virtually invisible to the unknowing eye. They have been traumatized by the event. Children are afraid to go out and play. Adults are afraid to take an evening stroll. People do not believe that the area is a major drug smuggling route, and they're uncomfortable with having Marines, who are trained to kill, on ground patrol in their backyards or flying low in helicopters that scare goats and people.

Normally when dealing with such traumatic events, the government sends in counselors to help people cope with the situation. But the town of Redford received no help. In fact, the government has not even apologized to Zeke's family. It has not admitted any mistakes, and has not cleared Esequiel of any wrongdoing. However, in January, 1998, it was announced that no charges would be filed against the Marine who killed him. Esequiel's family is filing a wrongful death suit against the government.

🌹 **Shirley Dorsey**
Driven to commit suicide
April 1, 1991

Byron Stamate, age 73 at the time of his arrest, faced the loss of everything he had earned in his entire lifetime as a civil servant when he was caught growing medical marijuana on his land for his long-term companion, Shirley Dorsey. She used cannabis to control her crippling back pain.

The prosecutor hounded them relentlessly with threats and planned to force Shirley to testify against her caregiver. Finally, it became too much for her to bear. Despondent over the prospect of not only losing Byron, but of ending up homeless and penniless in her retirement years, Shirley committed suicide on the first anniversary of the raid that ruined their lives.

The text of her suicide note read as follows:

"They want to take our property, security and herbal medicine from us, even though we have not caused harm to anyone. It is not fair or in the best interest of the people of society. I will never testify against you or our right to our home. I will not live in the streets without security and a place to sleep.

"I am old, tired and ill, and I see no end to the harassment and pressures until they destroy us. "

The prosecutor later said that if he had it to do over, he would still do exactly the same thing.

🌹 *Manuel Ramirez*

Age 26 at time of death in Albuquerque, NM in an early morning, no-knock drug raid in 1990, Manuel Ramirez was asleep on the living room couch in his home when Albuquerque Police Department (APD) Special Weapons and Tactics (SWAT) team officers and Navy SEALS approached his front door and rear windows to serve a search warrant looking for cocaine.

The APD officers, with the assistance of one or more SEALs approached the house and rigged a cable between the apartment door and a tow truck. Police broke out windows in the apartment's two bedrooms, including one directly above a crib where

a five month old baby was sleeping.

The crash of glass woke up a niece who ran from the bedroom and called to her uncle, because she was afraid the family was being robbed, the complaint says. Manuel reached for an unloaded gun just as the tow truck ripped the door off the apartment.

Police and SEALs burst into the apartment and shot Ramirez twice in the chest without announcing who they were, nor giving any order to drop the weapon before firing. Officers allegedly threw his wife and her niece to the floor, handcuffed them and then, for the first time, announced they were police.

Police found two marijuana cigarettes, a bottle with methamphetamine pills, and a spoon with drug residue in the search.

❧ Donald Scott
Killed in his home
October 2, 1992

Donald Scott was age 62 at the time of his death at his Malibu, CA home on October 2, 1992. He and his wife, Frances Plante, were awakened by a loud pounding at the front door of their house. As Plante attempted to open the door, a narcotics task force from the LA County Sheriff's Department burst into their ranch home, weapons loaded and in hand.

Above: Frances Plante mourned the death of her husband, Donald Scott, at a community memorial service in Westwood, California. Photo by Bill Bridges.

Plante was pushed forcefully from the door at gun point. She cried out, "Don't shoot me, don't kill me!" With a gun aimed at her head, she looked to her right and saw her husband charge into the room.

He was waving a revolver above his head. She heard a deputy shout, "Put the gun down! Put the gun down! Put the gun down!" As Donald lowered his gun, she heard three shots ring out, apparently from two sources. Her husband was killed instantly.

Scott was a millionaire who owned 250 acres of breathtakingly beautiful ranch land adjacent to federal park lands. Attempts had been made by the feds to buy the property, but Scott was not interested in selling. Claims that there might be pot growing on the land, made by agents who did aerial surveillance, were used to get a search warrant.

An official inquiry by Ventura County DA Michael Bradbury suggested that agents were hoping this raid would lead to asset forfeiture of the property Scott would not sell. His report indicated that taking the property was a major motivating factor in the raid.

No marijuana was found in their home or grounds. Scott did not even smoke it.

Below, inset: The coroner's office rendered a one word verdict on what the police did to Donald Scott: Homicide.

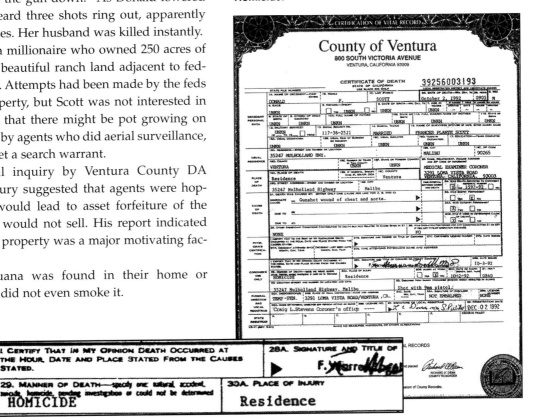

🌹 Jonathan West

Jonathan West was an AIDS patient and medical marijuana advocate whose death inspired his lover, Dennis Peron, and friends to sponsor San Francisco's Medical Marijuana Initiative of 1991.

Proposition P won with eighty percent of the vote, which led the way for the passage of Proposition 215, the California medical marijuana initiative of 1996, which passed by 56 percent.

🌹 Barb and Kenny Jenks

Kenny Jenks was a hemophiliac who contracted AIDS through contaminated blood in 1980. He unknowingly infected his wife, Barbara. Both became too sick to work, and they lived on disability. They discovered and used marijuana to help them eat and gain strength following chemotherapy.

Following their arrest, their lawyer argued in court that this was a case of medical necessity. The prosecution agreed and noted that they would die if they did not use it. After a lengthy legal struggle that sapped their strength, the DEA allowed them into the federal 'Compassionate IND' program, which provides some patients with six pounds of marijuana per year for medical use. The Jenks went public with their story, and soon more than 300 other AIDS patients had applied to the program.

More than 30 of these had successfully proven their medical necessity and were approved through the proper channels when the Bush Administration abruptly shut down the intake program in 1992. Even those who had already been approved were denied access to the medicine, and only the few patients who were previously receiving government marijuana at that time have been allowed to continue to do so.

Once again, people who had attempted to obey the law found themselves with no legal recourse to get their necessary medicine.

There was a huge outpouring of patient requests to the Jenks to try to help, but they were powerless to do anything about it. Their crusade for justice and compassion had been wiped out at the moment of its triumph. The stress of their personal ordeal from arrest, prosecution and legal battle, to this final, abrupt, arbitrary and irrevocable change in the federal 'rules' regarding medical marijuana all took their toll on the infirm couple's health.

Frustrated and depressed, the Jenks took a turn for the worse, and both Barb and Kenny died soon after the IND program was terminated.

🌹 Scott W. Bryant

Age 29 at his time of death when he was shot by police in Beaver Dam, Wisconsin on April 28, 1995. Scott Bryant was unarmed and did not resist arrest in any way. Police with a no-knock warrant charged through the door of his home and shot him down. His seven-year-old son watched his father die, while an ambulance took 35 minutes to arrive.

Police later reported finding less than three grams of marijuana (enough for a few cigarettes). Police claim it may have been an accidental shooting.

🌹 Chad MacDonald

When told he was facing a lengthy jail sentence after being arrested with about a half ounce of methamphetamine, seventeen year-old high school student, Chad MacDonald, agreed to act as an informant for the Brea Police Department in California.

The pressure he was under to make a buy large enough to satisfy the police and avoid prosecution on his charges led directly to his torture and death at a suspected drug house on March 3, 1998 and the rape and shooting of his sixteen year-old girlfriend, who had accompanied him. Revenge was alleged as the motive in court documents filed on two suspects who were arrested for the attacks.

Following assurances that her son would not be in danger if she agreed to allow him to act as an informant as they proposed, his mother, Cindy, signed the department's release form. This allowed Chad to go home. At that time, she was unaware that the arrangement involved Chad wearing a wire while making a buy until after one had taken place. Chad had confided in his mother that he felt pressured to make increasingly larger buys and that detectives had said his three previous undercover buys were not enough to make his legal problems go away. Mrs. MacDonald repeatedly told police that she had wanted him to end the arrangement.

Had she been advised that he could have qualified for a high intensity drug treatment program rather than faced hard time in custody, she would have jumped at it. Mrs. MacDonald believes her son would be alive today if the police had handled his case differently. Brea police deny he was working for them on the day he died.

Age 45 at the time of his death on August 8, 1993, Gary Shepherd was waiting at his home in Broadhead, KY, after a day-long, casual standoff that began that morning when a police helicopter flew over and landed outside the Shepherd home.

Officer:	*"Are these your plants?'*
Gary:	"Yes."
Officer:	*"We are going to cut them down."*
Gary:	"You will have to kill me first."

Gary was a Viet Nam veteran who had a crippled left arm from the war. Shepherd had deep convictions about medical marijuana, which he used to relieve his pain. He sat in a lawn chair guarding his plants for about six or seven hours, during which time no serious attempt was made to negotiate. Finally, Shepherd and his long-term companion, Mary Jane Jones, were ordered to put their hands in the air. As he raised his rifle to comply, police snipers hidden in a corn field shot Gary several times in the head and chest.

Gary Shepherd's four year old son, Jake, was sprayed with his father's blood and watched him die in the afternoon sun. Mary Jane Jones, the mother of his child, was grazed by a bullet of a Kentucky drug enforcement officer.

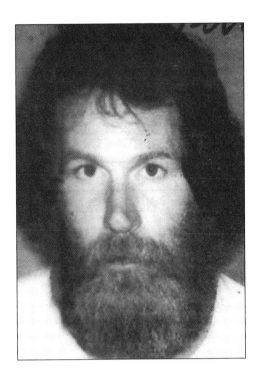

❦ Gary Earl Shepherd
Shot down on his front porch by police snipers
August 8, 1993

❦ *Gerardo Anthony Mosquera Jr.*

Age seventeen at his time of death from a self-inflicted bullet to his head in 1998. Gerardo Mosquera, Jr., a teen who took his studies seriously and worked after school to help support his family, became despondent when his father, a legal resident in the US for 29 years, was deported by the INS in December, 1997.

Mosquera Sr., 38, was sent back to Colombia, his native country that he hardly knew, despite the fact his wife and children were born in the US and he was gainfully employed as a forklift operator. His father's deportation came as a result of a crackdown on so-called "criminal aliens." His sole felony conviction stemmed from the sale of one $10 bag of marijuana to a police informant in 1989. As this law bans people from ever returning to the US, he was even denied permission to return for his son's funeral.

❦ *Unknown victims*

How many other patients die due to a lack of marijuana or other necessary medicines?

How many people are killed in drive-by shootings caused by the inflated prices of illegal drugs? How many die due to contaminated drugs due to the criminal underground market? The answers to these questions are not known, but the lives lost are no less precious to us.

Life. It's a human right.

The Drug War is not healthy for children and other living things

A horse's tale

✿ Easy the horse

Easy was the healthy animal seen on the left, until low-flying, marijuana-seeking helicopters spooked him, as seen on the right, causing injuries that forced his owners to put him down.

On June 23, 1994, Cheryl Humphrey went to look at a black stallion, named Easy, that she was interested in trading for her filly. Easy had just gotten new shoes, and she rode him for about 30 to 40 minutes. He was calm and gentle, healthy and not nervous or skittish. Easy was a beautiful horse.

Cheryl decided that if the horse passed the vet check she would make the trade. The vet did all kinds of tests (including blood tests) that showed no lameness, and advised her that he saw no reason not to buy Easy.

That July, she took Easy to her ranch in Humboldt County, California. Easy was getting adjusted to his new home and the other horses, when the Drug War paid a visit. Two Humboldt County Marijuana Eradication Team helicopters came to her ranch and started circling her horse pasture.

The other horses were somewhat accustomed to this activity, but Easy wasn't. He began to run frantically and call loudly. He ran and slid into the corners of the fence, touched the electric tape, spun around, and hit his head on the fence posts.

Meanwhile, the helicopters circled repeatedly over the pasture and the clearing, at times so low that Cheryl couldn't see it behind the tops of the trees. When she was finally able to catch Easy and calm him down, she cleaned his bleeding head wound and noticed that he was limping.

Cheryl kept a close eye on Easy over the next week. The next day he had developed a lump on the side of his forehead, and he continued to limp. A few days later, his right hind leg became so swollen that he began to hop around on three legs. X-rays revealed that his pastern (the area just above the hoof) had been shattered into five pieces and became infected. On August 6, 1994, the vet believed that there was little hope for Easy's recovery and they put Easy to sleep as a result of the flyover.

"Although we only had Easy in our family a short two weeks, we felt as though it was his whole life and we feel we were robbed senselessly of his last years. A person should never have to know what it is like to have to take your own friends life," said Cheryl.

Requiem for a Jail-House Kitty

A lonely stray kitty began coming into an inmate's room at night to keep warm. We wondered at the kitty's intuition of those he could trust. He hid from guards, yet befriended selected inmates. Our quiet, nurturing companion created a unique bond between informed prisoners.

The guards got wind of the infraction and launched a two week investigation into the incident, i.e.: ongoing surveillance, tactical meetings, capture strategy and raid-ing schedules. At 1 AM in the morning the SORT Team raided the inmate's room taking him by surprise — and into custody. True to form, when they attempted to nab the cat, our jail-house kitty thwarted their best efforts to capture him. Eluding the team, he darted between legs, climbed over and under beds, and finally leaped through an open window only to come face to face with the surrounding squad of men determined to make their 'collar'. Yet even this obstacle did not deter our kitty's dash to freedom. After another unsuccessful Marx Brothers chase, the slippery feline was seen as a blur streaking off into the night, evading the highly trained and expertly honed skills of the SORT Team.

Cuffing up the guilty inmate, they gathered the only evidence left; a saucer of milk and a little bit of food left over from the kitten's evening meal. This being what we refer to as circumstantial evidence, and not admissible for testimony, the guards were enraged over their failure to capture the evasive and now fugitive feline.

This morning when we got outside we found our kitty laying on the grass, poisoned. We grieve the loss of our small friend who was found guilty of sharing love, warmth and affection in this harsh, cold environment.

God bless that kitty.

-- Anonymous POW, May 1995
Sheridan Federal Correctional Institution

"What is happening in my country I did not want; I did not ask for it. The Great Father in Washington spoke to his children, and they set their dog-soldiers against us. They acted as though they had neither heads nor hearts.

"I lived peacefully and took care of my children. I committed ill acts toward no man. But they say we are bad. They took our homes and our lands that belonged to our fathers and their fathers before them. We did not wish to give even a part of it to the Great Father.

"The soldiers frightened our women and children. They took us from our children and put us in their prisons. Our old women wept and I thought I should cry, but then I remembered that I was a man. Our dreams died, and my heart was heavy; there was no hope and it seemed the Great Spirit had forgotten us. I am tired; my heart is sick and sad.

"Hear me, my friends, these are my words. When history looks back upon these bitter times it will say: 'This Drug War is wrong.' We are not dogs, we are men, and from where the sun stands, we will fight forever."

— Steve Tucker, Drug War POW, 1995

"Icarus Falling." by J. Clark, Deadhead POW. Color pencil and crayon. 1993.

Portraits From America's Drug War

The Drug War has no age limits.

Upper left: Shaunessy Sylvester, age 27 serving 20 years, charged with conspiracy to distribute crack cocaine.

Upper right: Loren Pogue holds his grandson. Age 64, serving 22 years, page 15.

Bottom: Cory Stringfellow with his parents. Age 29, serving 16 years, charged with LSD trafficking.

Previous page:

Left: Michael Clark with his girlfriend, and son, Malik. Age 28, serving 13 years, page 29.

Upper right: Amy Pofahl, age 37, serving 24 years, page 10.

Lower right: William Stonner with Susan, Danielle and Olivia. Age 40, serving 10 years, page 6.

It breaks up
African American families.

Above: Stanley Huff with his sons, Quentin and Xavier. Age 56, serving 15 years, page 17.

Upper right: Kevin Alexander and sons. Age 36, serving 20 years, charged with possession with intent to distribute crack cocaine.

Lower right: Danielle Metz and her children, Carl and Glennisha. Age 31, serving 3 Life sentences plus 20 years, page 13.

Women are the fastest growing part of the prison population.

Upper left: Veronica Martinez, age 44, serving 19 years 6 months, charged with conspiracy to manufacture and possess methamphetamine with intent to distribute.

Lower left: Zita Cullinan, age 62, serving 15 years, charged with conspiracy to distribute methamphetamine.

Above: Robin Roths, age 35, serving 13 years, charged with conspiracy to distribute methamphetamine.

Facing page:

Upper left: Shirley Womble, age 51, serving 25 years, charged with conspiracy to distribute marijuana (firearms enhancement due to possession by a co-defendant).

Upper right: De-Ann Coffman, age 27, serving Life plus 5 years, charged with conspiracy and possession with intent to distribute crack cocaine, aiding and abetting.

Lower left: Deborah Mendes, age 41, serving 12 years and 7 months, page 44.

Lower right: Valerie Johnson, age 33, serving 10 years and 1 month, page 20.

The Drug War is a war on people.

Upper left: Alfreda Robinson, age 43, serving 10 years, page 55.

Upper right: Nancy Simmons and son, Jason. Age 40, serving 10 years, page 45.

Lower left: Beverly Powell and daughter Tymisha. Age 42, serving 22 years, page 7.

Facing page:

Upper left: Anita Gage with son, Correy, and daughter, Melody. Age 48, serving Life, charged with conspiracy to aid and abet manufacturing of methamphetamine.

Upper right: Tracy Dina Ivy, age 27, serving 30 years charged with conspiracy to possess with intent to distribute, distribution of crack cocaine.

Bottom left: Kay Tanner, age 56, serving 10 years, page 11.

Bottom right: Therese Crepeau (right) with her cousin, Paula. Age 29, serving 28 years, charged with conspiracy to possess and distribute cocaine and cocaine base.

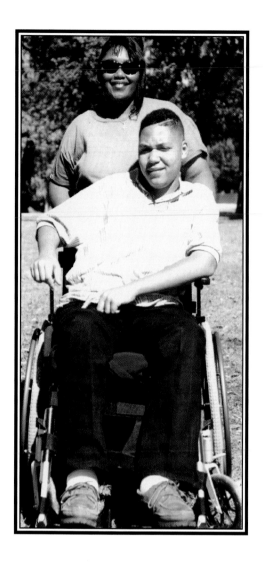

The Drug War tears families apart.

Upper left: Mary Jane Fike and son, Marlin. Age 45, serving 10 years, charged with conspiracy to distribute crack cocaine.

Lower left: Robin Norie and his daughter, Candace. Age 43, serving 15 years, 8 mos., charged with manufacturing, possession with intent to distribute methamphetamine.

Above: Everett Gholston with his wife, Brenda, and son, Everett IV. Age 40, serving 12 years 7 months, page 27.

Below: Mark Printz and family. Age 33, served a 5 year sentence, page 35.

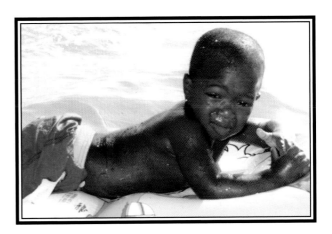

Leaving children behind

Upper left: Jacquie Fogel's daughters, Roezanna and Joni.
Upper middle: Jodie Israel and Calvin Treiber's daughter, Laura.
Upper right: Michael Clark's son, Malik.

Center left: Corey Woodfolk's son, Jamie, and friend.
Above: Hamedah Hasan's daughters, Kasaundra and Ayesha.
Lower left: Carol Cohn's twins, Jasmin and Jesse.
Below: Nancy Simmon's twins, Santana and Angel.

See index for pages of their stories.

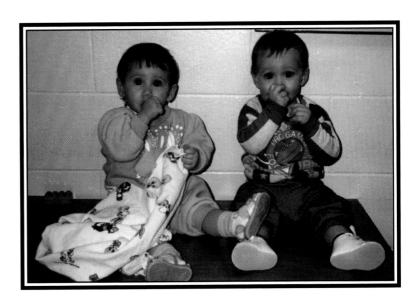

Suffering the anguish of separation

Upper left: Ernie Montgomery, with Ernest Jr. and daughter, Judith. Age 52, serving 11 years, 3 months, charged with conspiracy to distribute marijuana.

Above: Kevin Mauerman and daughters, Lacey, Summer and Julie. Age 36, serving 15 years 8 months, charged with conspiracy to distribute cocaine.

Center left: Scott Walt with wife, Dawn, daughter, Taylor, and son, Michael. Age 39, serving 24 years 6 months, page 54.

Lower left: Kim SaeLee and children, Nick, Nancy, Linda and Danny. Age 34, serving 10 years, page 46.

Below: Lovetta Clark and children, Stanley and Kaniesha. Age 43, serving 30 years, page 47.

Putting patients and their caregivers under attack

Above: Dennis Peron, founder of the San Francisco Cannabis Buyers Club. Awaiting trial, charged with distribution of medical marijuana, page 91.

Below: Valerie Corral, defended her cultivation and use of medical marijuana to control her epilepsy, page 83.

Upper right: Will Foster with wife, Meg, and children, Sarah, Josh and Anna. Rheumatoid arthritis patient, age 40, serving 93 years for medical marijuana cultivation, page 84.

Engaging in cultural suppression

Upper left: Jodie Israel and Calvin Treiber with their daughter. Ages 35 and 38, serving 11 and 29 years, respectively, for marijuana conspiracy. 'Operation Reggae North,' page 72.

Upper right: Lexi Bauer, age 25, serving 11 years, charged with marijuana conspiracy. 'Operation Reggae North.'

Below: Deadheads pose for a group shot in Federal Corrections Institution, Raybrook NY. 1995. 'Operation Dead End,' page 78.

Inset: Uncle Dead, drawn by a Deadhead Drug War POW.

VII.
Persecution by Prosecution

People from around the world flee to the United States to escape political and religious persecution and to pursue cultural freedom. The 'American Dream' is seen to not only include a high standard of living materially, but also a high standard of freedom.

Article 18 of the Universal Declaration of Human Rights states, "Everyone has the right to freedom of thought, conscience and religion: This right includes freedom to change his religion or belief, and freedom, either alone or in community with others and in public or private, to manifest his religion or belief in teaching, practice, worship and observance." The US Constitution First Amendment says "Congress shall make no law respecting an establishment of religion, or prohibiting the free exercise thereof".

How is it that so many churches are banned from practicing their sacraments and many political dissidents and social subcultures are routinely rounded up and locked away in the Land of Liberty? The Drug War.

When Congress adopted the Religious Freedom Restoration Act to protect the traditional peyote rituals of the Native American Church from the Drug War, it was overturned by the Supreme Court. When the late Dr. Timothy Leary sought to use LSD for spiritual purposes, that was forbidden.

The federal government disallows sacramental use of marijuana, despite the fact that people have used cannabis as a sacrament for thousands of years — at least since the ancient age of Zoroaster and in Egypt's

"In captivity." Ink drawing
Calvin Treiber, Rastafarian and Drug War POW. 1993.

"To prove a historical conspiracy, you don't need any marijuana. ... There can be just a slight connection to the conspiracy. But if it is a knowing — if you have known of the conspiracy, it is a knowing connection. That connection need only be silent to put them into the conspiracy itself."
— *Asst. Atty. James Seykora, US prosecutor against Jodie Israel in 'Reggae North' case.*

Jodie Israel

age 34, serving 11 years
charged with marijuana conspiracy

Calvin Treiber

age 38, serving 29 years
charged with marijuana conspiracy

Jodie Israel was indicted along with her Rastafarian husband, Calvin Treiber, and 24 others for an alleged ten year marijuana conspiracy in Billings, Montana. The FBI called its investigation 'Operation Reggae North,' since most of the defendants were Rastafarians.

Jodie was charged with possession of less than two ounces of marijuana, an alleged sale of four ounces (of which there was no evidence), money laundering, and conspiracy to sell larger amounts of marijuana. Jodie and Calvin are first-time, non-violent offenders. They believe their case to be one of political harassment and selective prosecution, as it is aimed at the distinctive cultural group — Rastafarians, who believe that smoking 'ganja' is a religious sacrament which brings them close to God. Meanwhile their four children, who range in age from fifteen years down to 6-1/2, have been virtually 'orphaned' by the government, since their mother and father are now locked away from them, serving long, mandatory minimum prison sentences.

"I have four children who all live with family, but in separate homes and towns. My oldest son, who is six, lives with my husband's mother. My husband draws beautiful pictures and my six year old son keeps each and every one of them in a box, three years worth. One night, he asked his grandma if he could sleep with the box. She went into his room later, and he had fallen asleep with his arm over the box... the only real part of his father he knows.

"It is so hard to explain to a child why you can't be with them and I believe it puts a tremendous burden on their little hearts. I feel these sentences are for the entire family not just the inmate. ... It is not just the prisoners doing time, it is our families, too. I believe it is just as hard on them as it is on us."

—Jodie Israel

"We as adults should realize marijuana should not be even put in the same category as hard drugs — herb is a naturally-grown plant and has not been processed by man into some incredibly potent chemical drug. It is far less harmful for people than alcohol or cigarettes that the government condones and sells. I've never seen or even heard of anyone dying from smoking marijuana. So why take people's lives and put them in prison forever for it?"

— Calvin Treiber

Above: Jodie with their children Richard, Tracy and Laura, in a 1997 visit.

Calvin holding their son Calvin Jr.

Freedom of assembly: Police almost outnumbered activists at this Florida cannabis reform rally. In many cases, authorities first attempt to block the permit to prevent the demonstration, then charge exorbitant 'use fees' or require them to post huge insurance bonds. Event organizers are sometimes later billed for 'police protection' services to pay for the officers' hours spent harassing and ticketing participants. The US Constitution First Amendment guarantees, "Congress shall make no law ... abridging ... the right of the people peaceably to assemble and to petition the government."

The Partnership for a Drug Free America is a tax-exempt propaganda organization that gets paid to produce biased and defamatory images of cannabis users. Radio, television, and the print media all oblige them with free air time to turn public opinion against all drug users. If it targeted any other subculture, such talk would be called bigotry. In America, it's openly promoted as 'zero tolerance'.

As Robert Riley, serving a life sentence without parole for an LSD offense, wrote, "It's not a war on 'drugs' you see, it's a war on individuality — on free thought, on a person's ability to refine within him/herself the concept of a higher power that may or may not go along with current standardized religion based 'dominator' societal dogmas! ... I'm not a PoWD (Prisoner of the War on Drugs), I'm a political/religious prisoner of an Inquisition that has been going on since 1100 BC."

Modern cannabis consumers share common rituals, such as passing joints around in a circle, and specialized language, two signs of social culture. They produce music, art and literature, the foundations of culture and civilization. Many hold life, spirituality and ecology in high regard. Most are productive members of society. Use of pot is an archetypal example of "Pursuit of Happiness." Some consider their marijuana use as a form of nonviolent civil disobedience. The Boston Tea Party; the civil rights movement; history is filled with examples of people risking jail to fight for freedom and justice. Some see themselves as patriots in the true spirit of the American Revolution. Every year hundreds of political rallies are held calling for an end to cannabis prohibition, and recent rallies in Atlanta, Seattle and Boston have reported more than 50,000 persons attending.

A pattern of political harassment emerges. Drug tests especially target cannabis smokers. MTV censors video images of the cannabis leaf but allows images of violence. Smoking utensils are banned and their presence cited as probable cause for police search and seizures. A prosecutor in Hawaii indicted political activists Roger Christie and Aaron Anderson and specifically told news media it was because the two had advocated cannabis reform. The charge: possession of *legal* hemp birdseed. Police in Alabama arrested the owners of a small hippie-style shop, Bohemian Rhapsody, for selling *legal* hemp products, in an attempt to force it out of business. The charges were finally dropped, but other examples abound.

Mary Yeager, age 42, and her husband, Jeff, were each sentenced to five years for conspiracy to distribute marijuana and LSD. She wrote, "My story is basically another conspiracy horror story. We own our house in the woods, with only electric to pay for (we have spring water, wood burning heat), and grew our food. We lived a quiet, secluded life and didn't flaunt our lifestyle, which included smoking marijuana. I think the federal government put us in jail because they didn't approve of our lifestyle."

Deadheads, psychedelic prisoners

The culture surrounding the use of LSD, peyote, psilocybin mushrooms and other psychedelics does not involve other criminal or any violent activity. For the most part, psychedelic citizens are non-violent and peace-loving. The vast majority of those incarcerated are serving long sentences for their first offense.

The Grateful Dead was a band that played psychedelic music from the days when LSD was legal and was sold on large sugar cubes. For some fans, 'acid' has been part of their passage into an inner realm of Deadheads; those who share a unique experience in an atmosphere of intimate trust. This reputation, plus its casual acceptance of odd behavior in a funky marketplace of drugs and art, made this group an easy target for sting and entrapment operations.

It is widely believed that Deadheads were targeted by the DEA beginning in the late 1980s as 'Operation Dead End,' and undercover agents were disbursed in large numbers to infiltrate the community. Although the Department of Justice denies the existence of such an operation, there is a clear pattern of Deadheads being prosecuted/persecuted because of their lifestyle choices.

Aaron Taylor (left)
serving 10 years
charged with LSD conspiracy

Todd Davidson (right)
serving 10 years
charged with LSD conspiracy

As mentioned before, LSD offenders routinely serve mandatory sentences based on the weight of the paper or carrier, not the the actual drug content.

A defendant's 'alternative lifestyle' is often presented during trial as evidence for conviction or for sentence enhancement.

In 1990 the DEA opened a San Francisco office for its recently formed LSD Task Force.

In some cases, agents spent years establishing trust with young people in 'Deadland' in order to entrap them into drug deals. In 1995 there were about 2000 Deadheads in federal prison for LSD or marijuana cases, serving anywhere from five years to Life. The taxpayers foot the bill for the LSD Task Force, plus an estimated $46 million per year to incarcerate these 2,000 prisoners.

Despite the adversity, many Deadheads maintain a positive attitude and even develop a sense of community in prison, expressing themselves through their artistic activities and communicating through the pages of their own publications, such as *Midnight Special*, founded by Heather Silverstein Jordan.

Heather Silverstein Jordan

served an 8 year sentence
charged with LSD conspiracy

"The US government seems to be embracing the methods of the late Comrade Stalin by creating a culture of informants. A society that turns friend against friend, neighbor against neighbor, and children against their parents is not a healthy one. I believe that this shall be their undoing. Only a generation ago, honor was a virtue, and today the state rewards deceit."

"We might remember that the War on Drugs is a new phenomenon. I reflect much on this as I sit in prison until the next century for a crime that did not exist at the beginning of this one. There was no drug prohibition in the 19th century. Certainly there was poverty and every other problem we know today, but drugs were not the cause and prohibition was not the solution.

"It is time to demand back our dignity as human beings. We should not have to ask the government for permission to put what we choose in our own bodies, nor should we need the state's fiat to buy and sell these things. Our homes and ourselves should be inviolate. We are not the property of the state, that it should protect us from ourselves.

"What do you suppose a man like George Washington would have said if the government had asked him for a cup of his urine, so they might be sure he was not getting into that hemp he was growing? Why should we tolerate it?"

In their own words

Pat Jordan

age 35, serving 10 years
charged with LSD sales

Deadheads Behind Bars

Dealt a little LSD
Ended up in jail
And I didn't hurt a soul
Don't want to be in this Hell.
Here I sit,
Even now I cry.
All I
Do is wonder why
Someone put me here.

Because I thought
Enemies were my friends,
Here they put me
In a world where happiness ends —
Not knowing love, or peace of mind
Don't even let me smoke 'The Kind'.

But all I do is hope
And pray,
Remembering that
Someday this will all go away.

— *Chuck Dean, Deadhead POW*

"Jer Bear in Chains." A symbol
of the Deadheads behind bars.
Color pencil and crayon drawing.
Unsigned, by a Deadhead POW.
1994.

Mark with his wife, Rosie.

Mark Misenhimer

served a 5 year sentence
charged with possession of LSD
with intent to distribute

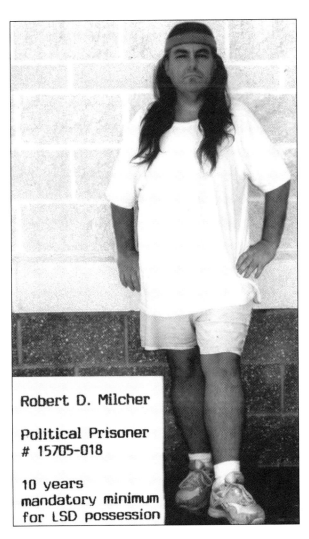

Robert D. Milcher

Political Prisoner
15705-018

10 years
mandatory minimum
for LSD possession

Free All Americas Drug War
P.o.w.s

R. J. Riley 59047-065
Conspiracy L.S.D.
Life w/o Parole or
11/4/93

Robert Riley

serving Life without parole

charged with LSD conspiracy

Lewis 'Skip' Atley

serving 20 years

charged with manufacturing psilocybin
mushrooms

In the Matter of Marijuana Medical Rescheduling Petition

"The evidence in this record clearly shows that cannabis has been accepted as capable of relieving the distress from great numbers of very ill people, and doing so with safety under medical supervision. It would be unreasonable, arbitrary and capricious for the DEA to continue to stand between those sufferers and the benefits of this substance in light of the evidence in this record.

"The administrative law judge recommends that the Administrator conclude that the cannabis plant considered as a whole has a currently accepted medical use in treatment in the United States, that there is no lack of accepted safety for use of it under medical supervision and that it may lawfully be transferred from Schedule I to Schedule II. The judge recommends that the Administrator transfer cannabis from Schedule I to Schedule II."

— *Francis L. Young,*
DEA Administrative Law Judge
September 6, 1988. Docket No. 86-22.

VIII.
The War on Patients

The intensity of the cultural war on certain drug users is so driven that, in order to send a strong message against social use of illicit drugs, our government even sacrifices terminal patients' access to beneficial medicines. Then it accuses those who support access to medical marijuana of using compassion as a 'stalking horse' for legalization.

It is a violation of human rights for a government to deny or withhold medicine from patients. It is an abuse of its power to hide behind a smoke screen of Drug War rhetoric.

'I feel your pain'

Doctors want to prescribe necessary medications, but are afraid to give adequate dosages of legal narcotic pain killers to chronic pain patients. They fear they'll lose their DEA license to prescribe any medicine. That happened to a Virginia doctor, William Hurwitz, which left hundreds of pain patients stranded. David Covillion killed himself when Dr. Hurwitz could not prescribe for him. Judith Curran went to Dr. Kevorkian when Dr. Hurwitz couldn't help her. The police took the medicine away from another patient after pulling him over, and threw him in jail overnight with no pain medications. He died the next day from the shock to his system.

The state Medical Board gave back Dr. Hurwitz's license in August, 1997. However, the DEA hasn't returned his registration number to prescribe narcotics so he cannot prescribe pain medications. As a direct result, another patient killed herself after a different doctor was afraid to prescribe adequate pain medicines, fearing retaliation from the government. The DEA should be held responsible for these deaths and its outright torture of some of the most defenseless members of our society: the sick and dying.

Medical Marijuana

Cannabis sativa, the scientific name for marijuana, has been used by physicians for at least 5,000 years. It is mentioned in the oldest pharmacopaeiae (medical books) ever recorded in China, India, Africa and Europe. A solid majority of Americans in polls today agree that patients should have access to medical marijuana. Scores of scientific studies, and tens of thousands of patient case histories and personal experience clearly demonstrate that cannabis is a safe and effective medicine. While cannabis may not directly cure disease, its smoked or eaten flowers have been found to be a safe and effective therapeutic adjunct to orthodox medical treatments, and as a stand-alone medicine for treating symptoms of many different conditions. However, the law does not even distinguish social from medicinal use of this herb.

Therapeutic Applications of Cannabis
include consumption of the herb for:

AIDS wasting syndrome, appetite loss, arthritis, cancer chemotherapy and radiation therapy side effects, chronic pain, cramps and muscle spasms, depression, epilepsy and convulsive disorders, glaucoma, insomnia, migraine headache, multiple sclerosis and spasticity disorders, nausea, PTSD, rheumatism, spinal cord injury, stress-related problems, vomiting, and many other conditions.

It is cruel and arbitrary to deny sick and dying people this effective medicine and it is inhumane to punish patients whose very quality of life depends on access to cannabis.

Denial of research

Cannabis is one of the most studied plants in the history of humanity and "one of the safest therapeutic agents known to mankind," in the words of DEA administrative law judge Francis Young. He ruled in 1988 that marijuana has been proven to have medical benefits for certain maladies.

Hundreds of studies have been done on cannabis. The British scientific journal *Lancet* reviewed the data and stated in 1995 that "The smoking of cannabis, even long term, is not harmful to health," and called for legal reform. The international Society of Neuroscience and the British Medical Association reported in 1997 that they had identified specific medical compounds in cannabis. The UN World Health Organization reported in 1998 that cannabis is safer than tobacco or alcohol, and there is still not one recorded death from cannabis overdose in medical history (aspirin kills about 1,000 people in the US each year). The *New England Journal of Medicine* in 1997 urged that doctors be allowed to prescribe marijuana. The National Academy of Science is conducting a review of the medical data, including personal medical case histories.

Despite all this, federal officials across the board claim that we need more 'recognized studies' before they can stop arresting sick people. The problem is that they also refuse to recognize existing studies and have blocked repeated attempts to do new studies. These officials have no such trouble, however, repeating sensational and spurious claims of alleged harm from marijuana, even though the claims are hypothetical and the data unproved or even known to be wrong.

In an ominous move in 1998, a group of Republican Congressmen asked the House Judiciary Committee to consider a bill asserting that no matter what the scientific research

shows, the US should criminalize and punish all cannabis use, medical or otherwise. They call it the "Sense of Congress". Actually, it's just more nonsense from Congress.

Getting medical marijuana

In response to the federal ban, legislatures in 35 states plus Washington DC have passed bills in support of medical marijuana. The problem is that they have no teeth and offer no protection to the patients, except in California where voters passed Proposition 215, which affirms the right to cultivation, but does not address how it can be distributed.

That leaves many patients out on the streets in the underground market, risking imprisonment and forfeiture. Despite their questionable status in California and illegality elsewhere, cannabis dispensaries, or 'buyers clubs,' have sprung up around the nation to provide patients a safe and consistent supply of medicine. Some, like California's San Francisco Cannabis Healing Center, The Green Cross Buyers Coop in Washington State, and others in Washington DC, Florida, New York, and elsewhere, have been harassed, targeted, shut down, and their staff members arrested and prosecuted for doing this compassionate relief work.

As of this writing, the medical marijuana issue remains volatile. Physicians can prescribe hard drugs — including cocaine, morphine, methamphetamine and barbiturates — but not this natural medicine. Patients are afraid to seek and use cannabis, and doctors have been threatened. The federal government is seeking to shut down California's cannabis dispensaries via an injunction claiming that the federal government has absolute power over the lives of all Americans, and disregard States Rights as well as human rights. In that case, the Court ruled that the right to life is not a fundamental right for Americans, nor is the right to medicine or freedom from needless suffering.

While some clubs continue to operate, the chilling effect is obvious. Armed, multi-jurisdictional anti-drug task forces have raided and harassed dispensaries, medicine gardens and even the patients themselves, ignoring the overwhelming support of the people that they be left alone. Medical marijuana providers have been charged with multiple felonies and are facing penalties totalling years behind bars for trying to help patients.

Urine tests are still used to single out and punish even legal users. California cancer patient Todd McCormick was arrested in 1997 for growing cannabis for his personal use. As part of his terms of release for bail, he has been forbidden to smoke marijuana, to use Marinol, or even to eat legal hempseed because it might affect his urinalysis. A patient in northern California was removed from a liver transplant list due to a positive urinalysis for cannabis. He was using it with a doctor's approval for pain, nausea and other side effects of his liver deterioration and the drugs used to control it.

Valerie and Michael's Story

Michael and Valerie Corral

Valerie Corral

epilepsy patient, caregiver

defended her marijuana cultivation

In 1973, Valerie Corral was involved in a freak accident that changed her life. A P - 51 Mustang, a converted W.W.II fighter plane, "buzzed" her car. The resulting accident left her with a head injury and a friend badly injured. Her injury led to an epileptic condition with up to five gran mal seizures a day.

Valerie tried using prescription drugs to control her seizures, but they did not work without devastating side effects. Her husband, Mike, read about experiments using marijuana to control seizures in rats. Valerie decided to try it. She went off the addictive drugs and began to smoke measured amounts and varieties of cannabis. She eventually learned to control the onset of seizures, using the herb alone.

For years, the Santa Cruz, California couple grew their own marijuana for her medicinal use. Then, in 1992, they were arrested. Seven and a half months later, Valerie's case became the first to successfully argue a medical necessity defense of cannabis in California. The district attorney told the sheriff he would not press charges if they were re-arrested. They planted again in the spring.

In 1993, six months after winning in court, CAMP officers came in force. Their home was ravaged and they were arrested. They acknowledged distributing cannabis to terminally ill patients for years. The sheriffs slapped them with cultivation charges, and also a felony distribution charge.

They reached out for community support. As a result of the efforts of Valerie and many others, Santa Cruz County voted to adopt Measure A, a resolution protecting medical marijuana patients. No further action has been taken against her since its passage.

Valerie has been appointed to the County Alcohol and Drug Abuse Commission. She is the founder and chair of the WoMen's Alliance for Medical Marijuana. WAMM became a Santa Cruz-based registered 501(c)3 organization for education and research for the provision of medical cannabis through propagation. It supplies free (or by donation) high quality, organically grown medical marijuana primarily to terminal patients who qualify with a doctor's recommendation. However, in the wake of the federal attack on the dispensaries, its non-profit registration has been revoked by the state. That 1998 decision is being appealed.

William Foster

Rheumatoid arthritis patient

age 40, serving 93 years

charged with marijuana cultivation

Inhuman treatment for an illegal medicine

Will Foster with his wife, Meg, and children (l-r) Sarah, Josh and Anna.

Will Foster was a productive citizen who paid his taxes, served in the US Army, and had his own computer programmer/analyst business for five years. He, his wife, Megan, and their three children were leading ordinary lives in Oklahoma until he was arrested for using his medicine of choice. "We were a happy, typical family that had a life and had dreams, but the Tulsa Police Department had different ideas," Will wrote.

Will has crippling rheumatoid arthritis in his feet, hips, lower back, and hands. He did not like the side effects of the drugs his doctors prescribed, which were mostly codeine-based and highly addictive. These drugs left him moody, tired and edgy, making it difficult for him to enjoy his family and perform his work. Will found that marijuana controlled the pain and swelling associated with his condition, so he grew his own medicine.

On December 28, 1995, based on a secret tip from a 'confidential informant,' police entered the Fosters' home with a 'John Doe' search warrant for methamphetamine. They found no methampheta-

mine, and no evidence of methamphetamine or anything listed on the search warrant. What they did find was his basement garden — 66 cannabis plants — and $28 cash.

Will refused to take a 'deal' and asked for a jury trial instead. However, he never had the chance to confront the witnesses against him, as the judge refused his Sixth Amendment right to do so. Furthermore, he was denied his Fourth Amendment protections against unreasonable search and seizure and nameless warrants. The prosecution poured on the pressure and the jury convicted him. He was sentenced to a total of 93 years — seventy years for marijuana cultivation, twenty years for possession of marijuana in the presence of a minor child (his own), two years for possession with intent to distribute, and 1 year for not having a tax stamp.

Since his incarceration, Will Foster has had very inadequate medical treatment, and he is suffering greatly. He now risks losing his left leg from the knee down, due to continued swelling that is inadequately treated in prison.

James with his wife Pat and their son Justin.

Right: James weight loss during incarceration took two corrective surgeries to allow him to regain weight.

James Cox

Cancer and radiation poisoning patient
age 50, sentenced to 15 years, served 5,
currently on 10 years parole
charged with marijuana cultivation

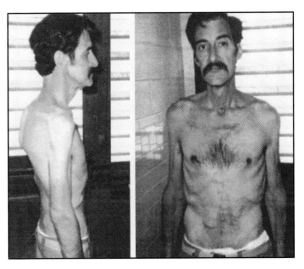

James Cox was introduced to medical marijuana following two operations for testicular cancer that had metastasized to his stomach. He found that it helped his pain, nausea, and eating disorders resulting from the cancer, chemotherapy and radiation therapy.

During his illness he was prescribed the narcotic, Demerol, which, in combination with marijuana, helped him cope with chronic pain from the nerve damage to his stomach, other organs, and ulcers. Marijuana also helped his inability to tolerate food and loss of appetite. James was on Demerol for fifteen years and became addicted. He found that if he increased his marijuana intake he could get off the debilitating Demerol and gain control of his life.

Since James could not afford to buy his marijuana medicine on the black market, he began to grow his own. Police discovered his garden while investigating an attempted burglary to his home. James and his wife, Pat, were arrested and the home they had just inherited from her mother was confiscated. James was sentenced to fifteen years behind bars, and Pat to five. Devastated and depressed, they attempted suicide while out on bond, but were discovered and saved. His sentence was given a stay and they were sent home. A free man, James' desire

to live returned, and he went back to growing his medicine. His health improved, but two years later, James was arrested once again on cultivation charges. This time they locked him away.

Lacking adequate medical attention in prison, he was near death. It took two stomach surgeries during his incarceration to keep him alive.

"Since I have been incarcerated and deprived of its use I have lived in constant discomfort which I feel is a direct result of not having the medical benefits of marijuana. My stomach deteriorated to the point to where I could not eat anything due to incurable bleeding ulcers," James wrote in 1995.

After spending almost five years in prison, James has finally gone home, but his government-enforced suffering is not over yet. James pain is intolerable and doctors concur with this. However, he will be on parole for the next ten years and will be drug tested twice a week for marijuana for the next three years. Doctors can, however, prescribe morphine for him. As a result, he has tested positive for opiate-type drugs. The state of Missouri is now threatening to send this patient back to prison for medicating his pain to bring it to a tolerable threshold.

Jimmy Montgomery

Spinal cord injury patient
originally sentenced to Life,
reduced to 10 years;
currently on medical parole

Ten years for two ounces of medical marijuana

Confined to a wheelchair for over twenty years due to an injury, paraplegic Jimmy Montgomery used marijuana to control spasms typical of spinal cord injuries and to stimulate his appetite.

Based on the testimony of an acquaintance who had been arrested for cocaine (and who received a lighter sentence for testifying against him), Jimmy was convicted of possession with the intent to distribute less than two ounces of marijuana found in the back of his wheelchair. He was also convicted in 1992 of possession of drug paraphernalia (pipes) and possession of two guns in the commission of a drug-related felony. The only evidence of intent to distribute was the testimony of an officer who claimed he had never seen anyone with two ounces who was not a major dealer.

The police attempted to seize the home in which Jimmy lived. Since the house belonged to his 62-year-old mother, Thelma Farris, she was also charged. After serving almost a year of his sentence and nearly dying twice because of the failure of the state of Oklahoma to provide adequate treatment for highly communicable diseases, Jimmy was released on an appeals bond in 1993.

On April 4, 1995, Jimmy was re-imprisoned. Rather than allow him to use medical marijuana, the government provided muscle relaxants, opiates and tranquilizers. He was in and out of solitary confinement, and handcuffed to a prison bed in Oklahoma without adequate medical treatment for the antibiotic-resistant infections in his lower body. Friends watched his condition deteriorate as the prosecutor blocked his release.

After considerable public pressure on Governor Keating, Montgomery was released on a medical parole.

Since leaving prison, Jimmy lost a leg from an ulcerated bed sore that his doctors were unable to cure. He is back working at the same business he had prior to his incarceration, a special engine mechanic.

Norm and Pat Major

Chronic pain and cancer patient
convicted felons on probation
charged with marijuana cultivation

Forced to plead guilty and pay a
$23,500 fine to save their family home
from forfeiture

Norm and Pat Major have three children and eight grandchildren. Norm, 60, is a former member of the board of governors at the Elks Club. Pat, 58, spends time working at the Altar Society at St. Peters Catholic Church. Because he "wanted a life," Norm and Pat Major have now become felons in Oregon, where state law does not distinguish between medical and non-medical marijuana use.

More than 30 years ago, back in 1966, an industrial accident in which a scaffolding fell on Norm's lower back caused recurring tumors to occur in his back. Two years later, as a result of painful complications, he was forced to undergo a hind quarter amputation, sacrificing a leg and half of his pelvis.

This was just the beginning of their long ordeal. In 1972, the cancer spread to a lung, which was removed. Recurring cancers, including a brain tumor, led to repeated surgeries. Medical records show Norm had more than 80 surgeries, including two to cut nerves to reduce pain. He built up tolerance for legally prescribed pain-killers. At one time, he required 600 milligram doses of morphine every three to four hours.

"I couldn't get out of bed because I was so drugged. I was more dead than alive. I took tons of stuff just to go to sleep." Addicted to legal drugs, Norm developed the temperamental behavior and physical symptoms typical of users of opiate-based street drugs. "I was a druggie. It was a nightmare." Pat agrees, "I had no life, either. It was all driven by Norman and the drugs."

Nine years ago, several doctors recommended that he try marijuana. The decision to do so was very difficult for the couple, requiring a lot of praying and crying, but they tried it and it worked. Marijuana made Norm's muscles relax which relieved the pain.

After a few months, Norm got off all of his prescription drugs. In the following years, he resumed his life, able to pursue hobbies such as refinishing furniture. To avoid the criminal market, the couple grew 36 cannabis plants in an indoor garden in their basement until an informant reported them to the police, leading to a raid and subsequent conviction.

"You have these people, who are otherwise pillars of their community, who were sentenced because he wanted a life," said defense attorney Rich Mullen.

Alan McLemore

**Alcoholism and
depression patient
age 46, serving 6 1/2 years
charged with marijuana
cultivation**

*After several weeks of
smoking cannabis, he
was not drinking at all.*

Alan with his wife, Maggi.

Alan McLemore had a reputation as a good lawyer until his relationship with alcohol began to interfere with his life. It was a long, slow slide downwards.

First, his legal practice began to suffer, then his wife divorced him. His life became a shambles, and his health gave out. From age eighteen to 39, Alan used alcohol to self-medicate for what was later identified as chronic clinical depression. An extreme eating disorder, painful migraines, drastic mood swings, and severe dysphoria are symptoms of his depression.

Drinking a half-gallon of 101-proof whiskey every other day, he developed alcohol-related gastrointestinal problems for which he was hospitalized on several occasions in serious condition. He sought out all kinds of legally available help: AA, treatment programs, psychiatrists, pharmaceutical anti-depressants. Nothing seemed to work.

Then, Alan started smoking cannabis. He found that by smoking marijuana before he took his first drink in the morning, he could somehow put off that first drink. After several weeks, he was not drinking at all. His life began to get back together. His law practice was growing. Although liquor had caused permanent damage to his stomach and esophagus,

his health also improved dramatically. He obtained a prescription for Marinol which he used when marijuana was unavailable.

Using cannabis to substitute for more harmful drugs, Alan began to garden on his land, producing cannabis to keep himself off alcohol and two others off crack, and to provide some friends with "safe, pleasurable entertainment." On February 8, 1995, he was arrested on charges of manufacturing marijuana. For a time, he was able to get his Marinol prescription from the jail psychiatrist, but not for long.

Alan has been sentenced to 6 1/2 years in a federal prison. Since Marinol is not on the Bureau of Prisons list of available pharmaceutical compounds (because it is classified as a Schedule II drug), he cannot get the medicine that most helps him.

The doctors have tried a variety of drugs that either do nothing for his illness, exacerbate his condition (causing significant fluctuations in his weight), or produce intolerable side effects.

Alan's weight has twice fallen to 120 pounds, and twice he has been rushed to a prison medical facility. As a result, his severe depression, loss of appetite, and suffering continue.

Thomas James Lowe

Crohn's Disease Patient
age 49, sentenced to 8 years, 3 months
charged with marijuana cultivation,
aiding and abetting

"I want to heal people with natural plant substances placed on earth by God for man's use for medicine."

T.J. Lowe was a photographer and naturalpathic physician who studied with the world famous herbalogist/iridologist, Bernard Jensen. He used herbs and plants to treat his own Crohn's Disease and to heal others.

Upon recommendation by a doctor at a VA hospital in San Diego, T.J. learned that cannabis along with licorice root extract and ginseng would relieve his cramps, nausea and loss of appetite. He began growing marijuana for himself and AIDS, MS, and glaucoma patients in San Diego, and trained and set up three other indoor growing systems. In 1993, the gardens were discovered. T.J. was arrested and charged with marijuana cultivation and aiding and abetting others.

He was sentenced to 87 months. Soon after sentencing, he was transferred to Terminal Island Prison where he was beaten by gang members who broke his nose, and confined to 'the hole' — a maximum security solitary lockdown isolation cell — for sixty days. T.J. was then transferred to Lompoc where he collapsed and required emergency surgery at Valley Center Hospital due to an intestinal obstruction from the Crohn's Disease. As this was not a prison facility, he was shackled and chained to a bed for 30 days and guarded by armed guards. The doctor who performed the operation recommended a second sur-

gery to remove twelve inches of his sigmoid colon, due to the danger of a rupture, severe diverticuli, and a mass found during the first procedure.

They decided to transfer him to the Federal Medical Center in Fort Worth, Texas to save money, but the doctors there refused to operate. They gave him heavy doses of drugs instead which caused liver damage. They took him off of those drugs, and now they refuse to give him medication for nausea and cramps to prevent further damage.

In prison, T.J. tried using cannabis to self-medicate and relieve the symptoms of his condition. In November, 1997, he tested positive for cannabis use and was subsequently sentenced to thirty more days in the hole. In 1998, once again seeking relief, he used cannabis but was discovered. This time he was sentenced to nine months in the hole.

When T.J. is released in 1999, he will have five years supervised release. If a drug test reveals that he is using marijuana, he will be sent back to prison. T.J. is hoping to benefit from California's Prop. 215 which allows patients to cultivate and use marijuana for medicine with a doctor's recommendation. As he is being held under federal jurisdiction, it is questionable whether he will be allowed to use it since the federal government refuses to recognize a patient's right to use marijuana as medicine.

Since he has been confined to prison, T.J. has lost his wife and all his possessions. He hasn't seen his children in over five years.

Elvy Musikka

**Glaucoma patient
defended marijuana cultivation
one of eight legal medical
marijuana users in the Federal
IND Program**

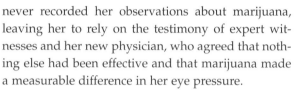

Elvy Musikka was arrested for smoking a government provided medical marijuana cigarette, even though her documentation proved it was completely legal.

Living in Florida, Elvy Musikka bought the Reefer Madness story, hook, line and sinker. As her already bad eyesight continued to deteriorate, she endured prescription pharmaceutical drugs which had uncomfortable side effects, but little effect on her glaucoma. Turning to ever more desperate measures, Elvy agreed to undergo a risky surgery on her better, right eye. The operation left her blinded in that eye. Only then did she consider suggestions to try using marijuana to reduce the buildup of inner eye pressure. To her grudging surprise, she found that it seemed to work.

Elvy discussed the effect with her doctor, and did her own experiments by eating marijuana brownies before certain visits to the doctor. His measurements of her eye pressure verified that the herb did, indeed, have the effect of lowering the pressure. Elvy began to grow her own plants and found that she was good at it; good enough to attract the attention of the police, who arrested her. She argued medical necessity and the judge agreed to hear the testimony. At this point Elvy learned that the doctors had

never recorded her observations about marijuana, leaving her to rely on the testimony of expert witnesses and her new physician, who agreed that nothing else had been effective and that marijuana made a measurable difference in her eye pressure.

The judge ruled in her favor, stating that Elvy "would have to be insane" to forego the use of medical marijuana. She was placed on the federal IND program, which provided legal marijuana for a few patients until it was shut down under the Bush administration in 1992. Elvy continues to receive government prepared marijuana cigarettes each month. Even though they are not as good as the medicine she grew herself, Elvy's vision has improved due to her steady use of marijuana.

Said Elvy, "How can I have a right to medicine but other patients not have the same right? I didn't lose my eyesight to glaucoma, I lost it to ignorance."

She is now an ardent spokesperson for cannabis reform.

Elvy holds her can of 300 IND issued joints that she gets every month.

Dennis Peron

'Pot Politician'
Founder of SF 'Cannabis Buyers' Club'
charged with marijuana distribution

"Join me in my quest for a more just and compassionate society."

After his military service in Vietnam, Dennis Peron came to a vision of a better America. He has been a political activist and pot advocate in San Francisco since the 1970s, and he has also been involved in advancing gay rights. In his never-ending quest to reform the law, he founded and operated Big Top, a marijuana supermarket that was closed down in the late '70s. He has been arrested many times and once ran for office while he was in jail.

Peron continued to fight for cannabis reform, inspired by the death of Jonathan West, his friend and lover, who used medical marijuana for his AIDS-related symptoms. Dennis helped collect 16,000 voter signatures to place the Proposition P: Marijuana as Medicine Initiative' on San Francisco's 1991 ballot. It passed with 80 percent of the vote.

That mandate, along with subsequent legislative victories and political endorsements, paved the way for the San Francisco Cannabis Buyers' Club. It was founded in the midst of the AIDS epidemic to alleviate patients suffering. The CBC provided a safe, cheerful environment for any patient who had been advised by their physicians to use medical marijuana. At its peak, the CBC provided cannabis for over 12,000 patients. Similar clubs were organized by patients nationwide.

The California legislature adopted two bills allowing medical marijuana in 1994 and 1995. Both laws passed by large margins, only to be vetoed by the governor. So, Peron, along with other activists, launched a campaign for a statewide ballot initiative, The Compassionate Use Act of 1996. More than 750,000 voter signatures were collected to put Prop. 215 onto the ballot. On August 4, State Attorney General Dan Lungren ordered police raids on patient clubs in San Francisco and Los Angeles. Both were local offices for the initiative campaign. When the Doonesbury comic strip ridiculed Lungren for his raids, Lungren called on newspapers to censor the cartoons. They did not. Voters went on to pass the measure in November 1996 by 56 percent.

As Health and Safety Code 11362.5, the new law allows certain patients and caregivers to grow or obtain cannabis for medicinal use. It does not change any other laws. A court battle continues as to the legal status of the patient cannabis dispensaries, but many providers consider it a moral obligation to continue dispensing the medicine to patients who need it, no matter what.

On Memorial Day, 1998, San Francisco sheriffs reluctantly moved on the cannabis dispensary and took control of the building, depriving 8,000 patients of their legal medicine, due to a court injunction. Dennis still faces criminal prosecution for his 1996 arrest, but took time out to run against Lungren in the Republican primary for governor.

For providing medicine to patients, Dennis is facing a lengthy prison sentence if convicted.

Is America caught in the quagmire of another Vietnam?

The parallels between the Vietnam War and the Drug War are many. Some Drug War equipment is even leftover from Vietnam, such as night viewing equipment, the helicopters used for fly-over surveillance in marijuana eradication programs, military transport vehicles, etc. Both wars have had hidden political agendas, profiteers and ill-defined goals.

It took former Secretary of State Robert McNamara 30 years to admit that the Vietnam War was a mistake. How long will it take the Drug Warriors to admit that the Drug War is wrong?

Vietnam War	The Drug War
Unwinnable war	Unwinnable war
Innocent civilian casualties	Innocent civilian casualties
Grassroots opposition	Grassroots opposition
Indistinguishable enemy	Indistinguishable enemy
"Search and destroy" missions	"Search and destroy" missions
Same villages won and lost	Same streets won and lost
Body count "victories"	Arrest & seizure "victories"
Dehumanizing the enemy	Dehumanizing the enemy
Fighting "Communism"	Fighting "Drugs"
$8.57 billion per year (average)	$16 billion in 1998 (federal only)
21 years (1954–1975)	26+ years and counting (1972– ?)
$180 billion total outlay	$??? billion (fed, state and local)

IX.
Drug War Industrial Complex

Once it is clear that a social or political policy is failing and has unacceptable side effects, why do politicians allow it to persist? It could be our fear of admitting a mistake — a key reason the United States continued its war in Vietnam for so many years after it was known to be unwinnable. Let's follow the money.

The Drug War has meant big budgets and profits for certain special interest groups. As mentioned earlier, it has been a big boom for the prison industry creating a need for more prisons, personnel, guards, and ancillary support services. It has meant bigger budgets for police and sheriff departments, federal and state government agencies. It spends money on military and interdiction efforts in the United States and internationally.

It means tax breaks for companies contributing to public relations firms like the Partnership for a Drug Free America to influence public opinion and demean drug users, as well as the DARE program to "keep kids off drugs." It has meant big profits for the drug testing industry to identify drug users and control the behaviors of the workforce. Even certain drug rehab centers have a financial stake in the Drug War because mandatory treatment required by some courts force people into their programs, like it or not.

> **"As federal spending approaches the one-billion dollar mark, establishing an entirely new 'drug abuse industrial complex,' no one has systematically analyzed either the problem to be solved or the solutions to be employed."**
> — *Report of the National Commission on Marihuana & Drug Abuse, 1972*

How would you like to come home to find this guy in your back yard? It happens in Humboldt, California.

The Drug War Industrial Complex has many tentacles and interests — too many to cover in this book. It is becoming increasingly institutionalized and entrenched in America. It s lobbyists take many forms, and its influence over policy makers is strong. A great expenditure of money keeps increasing without an accounting of the Drug War's effectiveness or its costs to society. It got a jump start during the Reagan Administration, but the Bush and Clinton administrations have kept it growing bigger and bigger at an ever quickening pace.

There is a price tag attached, however, and the total financial and social costs are extremely difficult to assess.

What are taxpayers getting in return for their money? More prison cells, fewer classrooms. Increasing rates of drug use. How much are they willing to spend to fight an apparently futile war? Can we afford such wasteful and ill-conceived priorities?

How much do we value our liberties and freedoms? How do you calculate the human costs of broken families and lives?

Militarizing the Drug War

President Ronald Reagan's election marked not only the turning point in the Drug War, but a radical reorganization of government. His top priority was to 'reduce big government' by implementing the largest package of budget and tax cuts ever. This was to be achieved in part by reducing and eliminating federal agencies. The Department of Justice (DOJ) resisted the plan, however, claiming to be the 'internal arm of national defense' and protector of domestic security. The Attorney General argued that having strong federal law enforcement would be a popular theme with the American people.

Thus, strengthening the DOJ became one of several exceptions to the rule of reducing big government. In the name of domestic security, Reagan could rationalize cutting essential social programs and giving that money to law enforcement, to get tough in the war on drug offenders and users. His crusade began with the requirement that every federal agency submit a 'drug budget' when requesting money. Dollars were most plentiful for those who were most willing to participate in the battle.

Although the US had been waging its war on drug users for almost two decades, drug importation was now portrayed as a threat to national security. International smuggling had not decreased, and domestic trafficking held steady. The DOJ and Reagan's advisors insisted there must be a clear and active part for the military to play in the fight against drugs, despite the 1876 Posse Comitatus Act, which forbade the armed forces from engaging in domestic law enforcement.

To build up the military's role in the Drug War, Reagan had Posse Comitatus amended

A national guard cannabis search and destroy mission wipes out somebody's cash crop.

in 1981, elevating drug policy to a 'warfare' status. Military forces could actively pursue and capture drug smugglers in US territories and waters. Airforce and Navy jets outfitted with elaborate radar equipment were sent on drug hunting missions. Other agencies like the Coast Guard were eager to act and took on drug interdiction as their newest goal.

Fueled by the sustained assault on drug offenders, by the late Eighties law enforcement became one of the top growth industries. The militaristic buildup continued as the DOJ formed multi-jurisdictional task forces that included the DEA, FBI, state and local police around the country.

With the end of the Cold War in 1989, the armed forces were freed up and therefore poised to contribute even more resources to feed the growing Drug War industry.

In 1991, Posse Comitatus was further amended to allow the military to train civilian police in counter-drug activities. In the nineties, the military has deployed troops along the US–Mexican border, and the National Guard has thousands of troops engaged in counter-drug operations. Currently, 89 percent of American police departments have paramilitary units — often trained by armed forces — whose most common task is to serve drug-related search warrants.

In 1998, some 66% of the Drug War budget is being spent on supply reduction (enforcement and interdiction) and 34% is being spent on demand reduction (education and treatment).

—*Office of National Drug Control Policy, 1997*

Above: a CAMP helicopter hovers below the legal 500 foot height limit over a farm in California.

Right: After a big raid, freshly cut cannabis plants are burned.

Summer CAMP in America

During World War II, the federal government subsidized farmers to plant a million acres of industrial hemp, mostly in the midwest. After the war, much of that cannabis went wild — known as feral hemp or ditchweed. During the 1970s this was tested and found to be a drug-free variety that served as ground cover, erosion control and birdseed. Around the same time, a national Campaign Against Marijuana Production (CAMP) was launched to extinguish cannabis.

Tax money has been poured into military groups like the National Guard, and into police budgets in all fifty states to search for and destroy plants. In 1997 alone, the federal government spent $9.24 million in its domestic pot eradication programs. According to the General Accounting Office, however, 99.28 percent of the plants they destroyed were not marijuana at all, but the feral, non-drug variety of fiber hemp.

In rural Humboldt County, California

The federal Drug War budget in 1969 was $69 million.

The federal Drug War budget in 1973 was over $800 million.

The federal Drug War budget for 1998 was $16 billion.

CAMP is active every summer and fall. Ed Denson, of the Civil Liberties Monitoring Project, reported that "Helicopter raids begin in April and continue until October. The choppers fly low over homes and gardens, often using the downdraft to blow trees around so they can see beneath them. The noise is overwhelming. Animals panic, birds' nests are destroyed, children are terrified.

"One helicopter can affect several hundred square miles in a day, and there have been as many as five of them in use simultaneously." There have been reports of hikers being held at gunpoint along backcountry trails, and vehicles containing heavily armed men turning up on private property. Many residents in these rural areas have complained that they feel like they are living in an occupied country.

This costly use of personnel and equipment is just one small aspect of the militarization of the US Drug War.

John Avery

age 58, serving 20 years

charged with conspiracy to manufacture marijuana, ongoing criminal enterprise, aiding and abetting, money laundering

"They basically killed my whole family."

In 1994, a fifty acre piece of land in the name of John Avery and his deceased son was raided by upwards of 75 DEA agents, local police and sheriffs in Kentucky. They reported that over 1250 marijuana plants were found in an underground grow room on the property. They arrested John's son-in-law, Ricky Daniels, and a friend, David Tapley who soon found out that they were facing many years in prison for their part in the grow operation.

The only way they could avoid long prison sentences was to testify and implicate others in a conspiracy. The government apparently wanted John Avery, and in order to charge him with being a leader of a 'continuing criminal enterprise,' they needed five names. Daniels blamed his wife, Michele. Tapley was able to get John indicted from a wiretap. For his efforts as an informant, Tapley was rewarded with $10,500 by the government.

They also pointed to John's other daughter, Sheri, and her deceased brother which satisfied the 'five' necessary to cut a deal.

Michele admits that her deceased brother (who lived on the property and was killed in a freak accident while repairing his vehicle three months prior to the raid) was probably involved in the grow operation, but she and the rest of her family claim that they knew nothing about it. No evidence was found to implicate them — no fingerprints (except John's on one piece of portable equipment), no plants, no pictures — just the words of Daniels and Tapley, who ultimately got off with the relatively light sentences of five years and two and a half years, respectively, for their cooperation with the prosecutor.

The Averys still maintain their innocence. John says he was a hard-working citizen who paid his taxes and owned a family business, Twin Lakes Drilling with one oil rig. He and his wife were saving up their money for the day that they could move from a basement home on an adjacent property they were living in for twenty years to the home they were building on the fifty acre property. The gov-

Above: Heavy military equipment was mobilized in the raid against this paraplegic and his family.

Left: Sheri with her son.

Right: Sheri, on left, with Michele.

Sheri Avery

serving 6-1/2 years

charged with conspiracy to manufacture marijuana

Michele Avery Daniels

serving 10 years

charged with conspiracy to manufacture marijuana

ernment confiscated the entire property and the two houses on it, one of which was almost built.

Though she is in poor health herself, John's wife, Eddie, has been left alone to care for her young grandchildren, Sheri's two sons, and Michele's disabled daughter until her daughters are released from prison. Michele now divorced from Daniels is serving ten years. Sheri is serving 6-1/2 years.

Says John:

"They basically killed my whole family. They took me and my daughters away from their mother, my wife, and their children, my grandchildren.

"Unless my attorney ... can overturn my conviction based on double jeopardy and several constitutional violations, I will die in prison considering my medical condition as a paraplegic, and my daughters won't see their children, who one of the children has hydrocephalus, for God knows how long."

Ryan Scheide

age 33, serving 7 years, 3 months

charged with conspiracy to distribute cocaine

"So in a nutshell, the drug war is not about saving the public from the evils of drug use and its distribution, as the politicians would have you believe.

"The drug war is about numbers. Number of dollars, number of prisoners, number of arrests, number of drug enforcement agents and a host of other numbers"

Ryan with his son, Jesse, and his wife, Amy.

Converting bases into prisons

Whatever happened to the 'peace dividend' that Americans were looking forward to at the end of the Cold War? Rather than cutting the military and using the funds saved to benefit taxpayers, the beneficiary of base closures has often been the prison industry. Marketed as a way of 'softening the negative effects to the community' from downsizing or closing a military base, the federal government has been using active and former military bases to house prisoners.

With infrastructure, water and utilities already in place, it is marketed as a 'convenient' and 'cost-effective' way to add bed space to the prison system. It also keeps federal dollars and jobs in the local area. It supports local businesses and services that provide such goods as building and hardware products, clothing, inmate commissary purchases (i.e. food, drinks, personal items, etc.), along with medical and hospital, laundry and trash, utilities, religious, psychological and educational services.

The Federal Prison Journal estimates that a prison institution can bring from 250 to 800 federal jobs to a community, paying an average salary of $26,000. With annual operating budgets of $12 to $30 million, it is no wonder

that communities are welcoming prisons to their areas. Duluth Air Force Base, MN; Boron Air Force Station, CA; and Webb Air Force Base, TX are a few examples of bases that are now known as FPC Duluth, FPC Boron, and FCI Big Spring respectively.

Urine the money

Another outgrowth of the Reagan era is the drug testing industry. Practically unheard of fifteen years ago, the testing of one's urine, hair, and sweat is increasingly being utilized to identify and punish drug users among the population. Drug tests do not detect impairment or performance, just the minute traces of drug-related metabolites in one's body. The American Civil Liberties Union decries this practice as a violation of the right to privacy, presumption of innocence, and freedom from unreasonable searches and self-incrimination. Furthermore, it is an invasive insult to human dignity. Nonetheless, mandatory drug testing without probable cause is a practice that is being used at an alarming rate, largely due to government mandates.

According to a national survey, about 44 percent of the workforce report that their employers subject them to some form of drug testing. Virtually all Fortune 200 companies impose it. A survey by the Chicago Sun-Times revealed that out of the ten largest private employers, nine drug test their workers. Drug tests are now commonly required for pre-employment screening purposes, and an increasing number of businesses, police departments, government agencies, prisons, the armed forces, and sports organizations have begun to jump on the bandwagon.

The developers of drug tests quietly lobby for more laws that force you to submit to their scrutiny before you will be able to get a driver's license or participate in school athletic programs. Widespread testing ensures huge profits for these companies. One of the largest such firms, Smithkline Beecham, sold over 24 million drug tests in just ten years. The company that holds the patent on hair testing, Psychemedics Corp., reported that its sales had tripled from 1992 to 1996 to $12.2 million.

While most people support the employer's right to forbid drug use on the job, the arbitrary nature of drug testing is obvious on its premise. Consider random drug testing; if an employee is performing their job so well that the only way their employer can tell if they have ever used an illicit drugs is to test bodily fluids or hair, they are doing their job. Their private lifestyle is not a work-related issue, so the employer has no inherent interest or right to invade the worker's privacy. If an employees' drug use keeps them from performing their duties, they can be fired without resorting to a urine test. So the test itself serves no purpose except to intimidate and dominate the workforce.

Technology available to hair testing companies can detect traces of illicit drugs up to ninety days prior to the test. As marijuana is the most common illicit drug detected through these tests, this could effectively prevent a person who has smoked a marijuana joint in the last three months from making a living! Further, drug tests are fallible. People can be banned from employment, lose custody of their children, or be sent back to prison for a parole violation — based on a false positive. This effectively penalizes peo-

ple, not for their impairment or performance, but at the whim of a flawed test that claims to show the presence of something in their bodies that the the government finds offensive.

Incarceration vs. education

A look at federal and state spending priorities reveal that politicians are choosing bars over books, making higher education another casualty of the Drug War. Prisons are competing with universities for government funds, and the students are losing. The Washington DC-based Justice Policy Institute reports that more money is currently being spent on building prisons in this country than on building universities.

Nationwide, state funding for prison construction increased by $926 million, while funding for higher education construction decreased by a similar amount. From 1987 to 1995, state prison expenditures increased by thirty percent, and spending on higher education decreased by eighteen percent during that same period.

California and Florida budgets showed more spending on prison systems than on public universities; a reversal from a decade ago. From 1984 to 1995, California built 21 new prisons but only one new university. For the annual price of incarcerating one drug offender, the state could educate ten community college or five state university students. The State of Texas has also followed this trend with a vengeance. Over the last ten years, 77 new prisons have been built at a cost of $2.3 billion, and only one university, costing $66 million. The prison population has increased by 104,000, to 143,000, while the university population has grown by only 35,000 students in the same period.

> Between 1985 and 1995, the number of adults in prison has jumped 131%, the number in jail has doubled, on parole up by 134%, and the number on probation by 61%.
> — *US Dept. of Justice.*

As a result of spending priorities, students are finding it more and more difficult to pay for their education, preventing many from attending college at all. A loss in education funds means students and their families must pay a larger share of their tuitions, burdening them with high debts from loans upon graduation. As Professor Skolnick of UC Berkeley put it, "Students are bearing the brunt of prison spending. When tuition goes up, they're not paying for better education, they're paying for prison guards or prisons."

Truth or DARE

Education takes another hit in the Drug War, this time in its credibility among students. Schools are forbidden to talk about responsible use of illicit drugs or give safety advice other than strict abstinence: 'Just say no.' How do they learn moderation or where to draw the line if they happen to say 'yes'?

Kids have become hysterical upon seeing their parents drink wine after being told that drinking alcohol is drug abuse. Kids whose parents smoke tobacco, drink alcohol, or smoke marijuana responsibly see the contradiction. Television bombards them with ads for beer and pharmaceuticals. Newspapers and magazines are fat with ads for liquor and cigarettes.

Just say what?

Universal Declaration on Human Rights Article 26.2 states, "Education shall be directed to the full development of the human personality and to the strengthening of respect for humans rights and fundamental freedoms. It shall promote understanding, tolerance and friendship." Due to 'zero tolerance,' children have been punished or suspended from schools for offering each other aspirin or throat lozenges. In 1997, a child was suspended for giving his French teacher a bottle of wine as a Christmas gift. A girl who offered a friend her inhaler during an asthma attack in 1998 was given a demerit on her record instead of being praised as a 'Good Samaritan' for possibly saving her friend's life.

A DARE officer plays with a child in Oakland, CA, 1995.

Started in 1983 by Los Angeles Police Chief Daryl Gates, DARE (Drug Abuse Resistance Education) is a grammar-school program taught by police officers that combines indoctrination with an expensive media and public relations campaign for police departments.

Present in 52 percent of US school districts, DARE receives some $750 million per year, mostly from federal, state and local taxes, but also from private donations and the

Federal taxpayers spend four times more money per year to incarcerate one Drug War POW — $23,000.00 — than we do to educate one child — $5,421.00!

California prison guards earn almost $10,000 per year more than public school teachers. An average prison guard with a high school equivalency diploma now earns more than a tenured associate professor with a PhD.

What kind of message does this priority send our young people on how much value society puts upon their education?

royalties from sales of its merchandise. DARE glamorizes drugs by having a uniformed officer drive to school in a fancy car confiscated from a drug dealer. Sometimes students are handed a letter to have their parents sign, promising a 'drug free home.' In some schools, lists have been compiled of who signed and who declined. Youngsters have followed DARE instructions and called '911' services to turn in their parents to 'help' them for having drugs. We see what form that help takes: the destruction of home and family.

These programs also violate the trust of the family itself. UDHR Article 26.3 states, "Parents have a prior right to choose the kind of education that shall be given to their children." Yet, when Leo Mercado held his daughter out of an Arizona DARE class, police raided his home.

Study after study — including one funded by the Department of Justice and conducted by the Research Triangle Institute in 1994 — shows that DARE is ineffective at reducing drug use among students, and may, in fact, lead to increased drug abuse. In recent years many local communities, including Oakland, California have decided to abandon the program. However, it still receives money and praise from officials at all levels of government. Though DARE may be counter-productive, politicians get blind satifaction from feeling like they are doing something for drug education, and police, looking for a way to improve community relations, love all the money and support it brings them.

The price tag

Over the course of his eight years in office, Reagan spent $22.6 billion on his revived Drug War. Another major escalation was pushed through under George Bush, who spent $42.5 billion in a single term. Under Clinton, spending has continued to increase, with $16 billion for one year alone allocated in the 1998 fiscal budget. Those figures show federal spending only, not counting all unfunded mandates passed onto states.

Spending at other levels of government adds up to approximately the same as the federal budget, so in 1998 you can expect to see well over $30 billion spent on the Drug War.

In 1999, the federal Drug War budget alone is expected to rise again to $17 billion.

Are we better off by spending more money on the Drug War? Where will it end?

Calculating Drug War costs

• **The average cost of incarcerating a federal inmate is $23,000 per year. (FAMM, Coalition for Federal Sentencing Reform, March, 1997.)**

• **Almost 60% of federal inmates — 55,624 people! — are drug offenders. Half of these are first time, non-violent offenders. (Bureau of Prisons, 1997.)**

• **To feed, clothe, house and guard these 55,624 prisoners costs taxpayers $3.5 million per day, or $1.27 billion annually.**

— **And there's lots more expense, such as —**

• **Public assistance or welfare for children of inmates who have lost a breadwinner,**

• **Foster care for children who have lost their parents,**

• **Unnecessary and inaccurate urine testing of employees, damaging both morale and job productivity,**

• **Medical costs to treat people for diseases spread by sharing dirty needles due to bans on needle exchange programs,**

• **Homes, property, cars, and savings forfeited from families of inmates,**

• **Money, property stolen to support expensive illegal drug habits,**

• **Money diverted from the open market to the underground market,**

• **Tax dollars and untaxed incomes lost to the black market economy of drugs,**

• **Tax dollars lost by giving tax-exempt status to Drug War propagandists such as: PRIDE, PDFA (Partnership for a Drug-Free America), Drug Watch International, DARE, etc.,**

• **Other criminal justice system costs,**

• **Hidden law enforcement budgets,**

• **Paid informants,**

• **Court costs,**

• **Attorney fees,**

• **Families destroyed and lives lost.**

Anton Edwin Hosch

serving 24 years

charged with marijuana
conspiracy

+

Steve Williams

age 44, serving 24 years

charged with marijuana
conspiracy , money laundering

=

x 20 years

Taxpayers will spend almost $1,000,000.00
incarcerating just these two marijuana offenders ...

That's enough money to educate about 20
community college students each year for 20 years.

California figures. Based on: *From Classrooms to Cell Blocks: A National Perspective.* Justice
Policy Institute, February 1997.

Federal funding in the 1998 Drug War budget *

Bureau of Prisons	$2.02 billion
Substance Abuse and Mental Health Services Administration	$1.33 billion
Department of Veterans Affairs	$1.18 billion
Drug Enforcement Administration (DEA)	$1.15 billion
Federal Bureau of Investigation (FBI)	$865 million
Office of Justice Programs	$815 million
Department of Defense	$809 million
Department of Education	$747 million
Customs Service	$641 million
Federal Judiciary	$621 million
National Institute on Drug Abuse (NIDA)	$549 million
Office of Community Oriented Policing Services	$510 million
US Coast Guard	$389 million
Immigration and Naturalization Service (INS)	$367 million
Office of National Drug Control Policy	$361 million
Health Care Financing Administration	$360 million
Interagency Crime and Drug Enforcement	$295 million
Department of Housing and Urban Development	$290 million
Federal Prisoner Detention	$281 million
US Marshals Service	$273 million
US Attorneys	$269 million
Bureau of Alcohol Tobacco and Firearms	$232 million
State Department	$214 million
Centers for Disease Control	$115 million
U.S. Secret Service	$90 million
Internal Revenue Service (IRS)	$73 million
Department of Labor	$66 million
Federal Law Enforcement Training Center	$61 million
Administration for Children and Families	$54 million
Health Resources and Services Administration	$48 million
Indian Health Service	$43 million
Corporation for National Service	$40 million
Food and Drug Administration (FDA)	$35 million
National Highway Traffic Safety Administration	$31 million
Department of Justice Criminal Division	$28 million
US Intelligence Community	$27 million
Federal Aviation Administration	$23 million
Bureau of Indian Affairs	$18 million
Special Supplemental Food Prog. for Women Infants and Children	$15 million
Financial Crimes Enforcement Network	$13 million
National Park Service	$9 million
US Forest Service	$9 million
Bureau of Land Management	$5 million
Agricultural Research Service	$5 million

* Proposed for federal budget only. Does not include state or local funding.

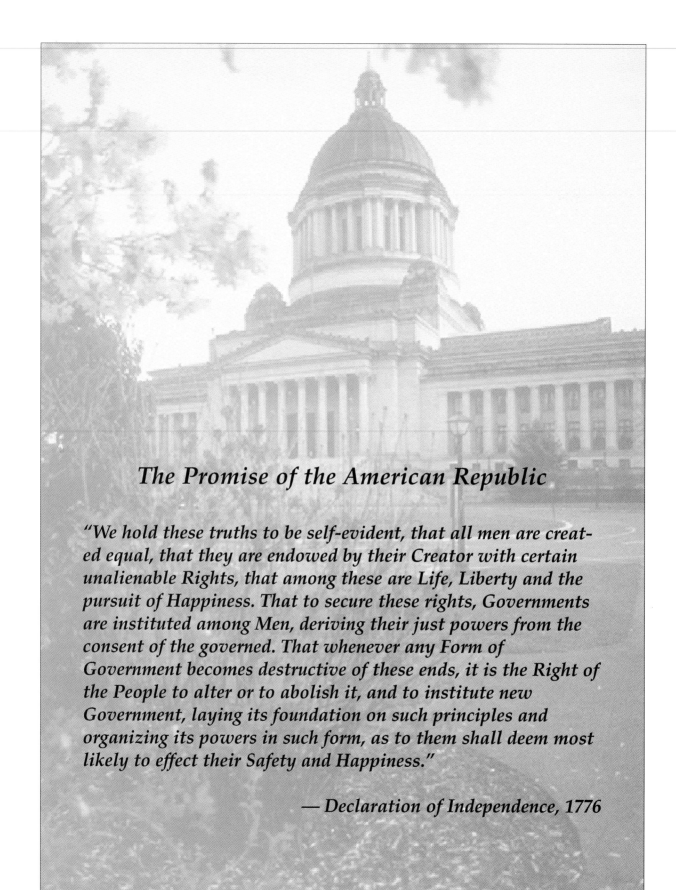

The Promise of the American Republic

"We hold these truths to be self-evident, that all men are created equal, that they are endowed by their Creator with certain unalienable Rights, that among these are Life, Liberty and the pursuit of Happiness. That to secure these rights, Governments are instituted among Men, deriving their just powers from the consent of the governed. That whenever any Form of Government becomes destructive of these ends, it is the Right of the People to alter or to abolish it, and to institute new Government, laying its foundation on such principles and organizing its powers in such form, as to them shall deem most likely to effect their Safety and Happiness."

— Declaration of Independence, 1776

X.

From War to Peace

These laws are not going to change, these people will not be released from jail, and the profiteers will not let go of the golden goose unless we all become part of the solution. Though it has never been easy to stand up to entrenched and institutionalized forces of power and corruption, there are many steps that can be taken to ease the suffering and find a more just resolution to the appalling situation revealed in this book.

First and foremost, it is time to open discussion and honestly assess America's drug policies. We must demand accountability from our politicians who are addicted to failed policies, and look for other models that work to protect human rights and lessen the harms associated with both drugs and the Drug War. We must get rid of the rhetoric that perpetuates injustice, and be creative in our approach to the drug problem. Too much is at stake to persist along the same, old path that only leads towards a further breakdown in America's democratic values.

It's time that we apply common sense to the drug issue and reprioritize our spending.

Opening the discussion

When asked at the Commonwealth Club of California on July 2, 1997 what his response was to those calling for drug law reform, the drug czar, General Barry McCaffrey, said "I would welcome that dialogue." It's time to hold him to that offer.

A national dialogue is called for that puts all the cards on the table and engages everyone, from all walks of life. In town halls, schools, public hearings, community centers, the workplace, churches, and the media, open debate must involve a cross-section of society — parents, teachers, students, doctors, health care and social workers, business people, workers, politicians, law enforcement, human rights advocates, the clergy, judges, lawyers, prisoners, wardens and drug users. This breadth of input is necessary to honestly assess the problems and find workable solutions. After all, we *are* in this together.

Asking the right questions

For an open discussion, asking the right questions will help us find good answers.

What are the underlying root causes of drug use and abuse? Why do people engage themselves in the drug market and commit drug offenses? If no one claims to be a victim, why is it a crime? How do poverty and the lack of economic opportunities affect people's involvement? What role does education play in all this? What can we do to prevent drug abuse? Would greater accessibility to drug and alcohol treatment or health care be more effective than incarceration in helping people with drug problems? What about people who use drugs responsibly? Should they have the right to use them, or should they have equal protection as users of legal drugs? What is effective drug education? What exactly are the 'compelling interests' to create a drug-free America? Is that even possible? How far are we willing to go to achieve that? Are we willing to sacrifice our treasured Constitutional protections and human rights to attempt it? What can we do to correct the injustices of our laws and policies? How many prisoners are enough? What new models can we adopt that protect rights and freedoms, and hold families together while lessening the harms associated with drugs and drug policy?

Let's move beyond the metaphor of war and hot rhetoric that perpetuates injustice, and replace them with metaphors of tolerance and community building.

We owe it to our youth to find a path that leads America from war to peace.

What is effective drug education?

Teaching children how to attain a healthy and successful lifestyle benefits everyone. Preventing adolescent drug use (including alcohol and tobacco) and promoting abstinence among children are goals that enjoy nearly universal support.

Yet, children easily obtain and experiment with illicit substances amid the Drug War, due in part to the ubiquitous, unregulated black market. Giving the false impression that all use is abuse leads to self-fulfilling prophecies that cause hysterical reactions, make mountains out of molehills, and encourage failure rather than success. Despite the best efforts to deter drug use, the reality is that there is a good chance young people will experiment at some point. It does not mean that they automatically have a problem, but they do have a need to know the facts.

If students get inaccurate information about one drug, they soon learn to distrust their teachers. Their logic goes, 'since marijuana wasn't as bad as they said, heroin must be okay, too.' But it's not, and they need to know that. Since not all drugs are alike, young people need to understand the relative risks and effects of using different drugs.

Honesty is still the best policy. In order for children to grow up and make responsible decisions, adults must give them accurate information and guidance. Propaganda-type programs based on scare tactics and indoctrination are less effective in preventing drug problems than are public health-oriented curricula that emphasize personal safety and responsibility. Children are smarter than that, and they can be taught that certain rights and privileges come with adulthood, and some

things are not for kids. As part of a health and life skills curriculum, effective drug education strengthens their ability to make good choices regarding various aspects of their lives and understand the consequences of their actions and the decisions they make.

Drug education begins at home. Parents who talk to their children and show by example how to responsibly manage their lives impart invaluable lessons to their children. If parents drink alcohol or have experimented with drugs (as a good many have), they must pass on their knowledge and best advice to their children. Hiding from and lying to them leads to a breakdown of communication and a breakdown in family relationships.

Studies show that most young people who get into trouble with drugs do so in the hours between 4:00 and 8:00 in the afternoon. Left unsupervised with nothing to do, kids often look for some excitement. After-school programs that provide interesting activities with adult supervision or parental involvement have been shown to deter drug use better than anti-drug programs do.

Opening the discussion on how to best serve our young people is an area that deserves exploration. Zero tolerance policies that go beyond drug education and expel troubled children from schools, randomly search lockers and drug test students have serious consequences that also need to be considered. What will happen to children who are cast out from schools? What lessons do children learn about trust when they are treated with distrust? How can we better help children attain success in their lives?

The human rights question

Article 1 of the UDHR states, "All human beings are born free and equal in dignity and rights. They are endowed with reason and conscience and should act toward one another in a spirit of brotherhood."

The Drug War treats our brothers and sisters, our friends and neighbors, our fellow citizens, as the enemy. The Drug War is a war on

A 1998 march through San Francisco to support California's medical marijuana dispensaries against a federal injunction seeking to close them. Proposition 215 legalized cultivation and use of medical marijuana, but did not create a distribution system.

people. If society is to manifest the "spirit of brotherhood," we must explore new ways to reach out to people with problems, and help them find ways of entering the fold.

Again, asking the right questions will help us find humane answers. How can we reduce criminality and create fewer criminals? Are our drug laws and policies just? Do non-violent drug offenders deserve longer sentences than violent criminals? If people are not a threat to others, do they belong in prison? Is justice being served by the Drug War? If not, what can be done to correct the injustice? Following are some suggestions.

Re-think policies, reform laws

As seen in this book, mandatory minimum sentences are clearly unjust. They have been tried and abandoned before, and it is time to repeal them once and for all. Families Against Mandatory Minimums (FAMM) is one group working toward that goal (see resource list in the appendix). At a bare minimum, sentencing disparities of a racist nature should be eliminated. If the quantities for crack were moved up to correspond more closely to powder cocaine, it would help reduce the disproportionate incarceration of African Americans. Discounting carrier weights and mixtures from the drugs would give a more accu-

rate assessment in determining sentencing. Making the sentencing 'safety valve' retroactive would give some relief to many first time, non-violent drug offenders who were sentenced prior to 1994 and are still in prison.

If drug conspiracy law adhered to the same standards as general conspiracy law, — where an actual crime is required to be committed to convict someone and hearsay evidence is inadmissible — chances of justice be administered would greatly improve. It would prevent people from being sent to prison for a lifetime based solely on the word of questionable sources.

Law enforcement is meant to stop crime, not create it, yet informants and undercover agents are paid to commit crimes and entrap other people into breaking the law. Why are they enticing people into crime? Shield laws that allow police to commit crimes corrupt the legal process and should be revoked.

Judges serve as instruments of justice in a free society. The criminal justice system was designed to have checks and balances. Judges are not prosecutors and their role is not meant to merely rubber stamp sentencing. They are supposed to weigh various issues and circumstances involved in each case, and allow defendants to fully present their cases — including motives — to defend themselves.

Judges must reclaim or be given back their discretion in the courtroom so as to dispense real justice on an individual basis.

Sentencing options other than prison time need to be explored for non-violent offenders who are no threat to society. How would society and the offender's family better be served than the costly and inhumane sentences of years behind bars? Shorter sentences, community service, residential settings that allow mothers to stay with their young children, parenting classes, treatment, home confinement, or probation are a few options. Don't they deserve a second chance?

The Justice Policy Institute proposes to "adopt a moratorium on new prison construction. Cut the non-violent prisoner population in half over the next five years." This proposal would force policy makers to be more creative in dealing with social problems while curbing and reversing the rising rates of incarceration. Again, what are other options to incarceration?

Conservative Judge James Gray of Orange County, California suggests that people be held responsible for their actions that impact or victimize others, rather than for drug offenses that have no victims other than the offenders themselves. Drug use need not be a crime for the user to be held legally responsible for their personal conduct. If anyone commits a violent or other crime, prosecute them. This would protect the public while dispensing equal justice to all citizens, and help to unclog the court system.

Prohibition is at the core of the Drug War. Prohibition is not keeping drugs off the streets or even out of the prisons. What are alternatives? Allow personal use? A regulated market? Legalization with controls? Access by prescription?

Many groups are working to end the drug prohibition which has created and facilitates an out-of-control black market. Many marijuana law reformers, in particular, are calling for a regulated and controlled legal market that protects children from access, but allows adults to grow, buy, and consume cannabis in appropriate settings. The majority of Americans agree that patients who need it deserve to have access to medical marijuana without prosecution. Some believe that the right to privacy allows people to grow cannabis and consume it in the privacy of their home. The private sector would be responsible for distribution, with age limits and regulatory controls similar to alcohol. It would be subject to taxes that could go towards education or other services.

By decriminalizing marijuana, many otherwise law-abiding citizens would no longer be considered criminals. That would be a significant start in restoring respect for the law.

Marijuana prohibition has also led to privacy violations by CAMP and other cannabis eradication programs. These programs have potentially devastating environmental effects due to herbicide spraying, and could be ended by de-funding them.

Protect property and privacy

Asset forfeiture laws that take people's personal property — especially innocent owners or those not convicted of any crime — are un-American. They lead to corruption and overzealous seizures as well as a conflict of interest for enforcement agencies whose budgets depend in part upon seized assets. The group Forfeiture Endangers American Rights (FEAR) works to reform these laws.

A search warrant should be required before any sweeps or surveillance. A higher standard of proof should apply before issuing such a warrant, and government ought to repay property owners for any damage its agents cause during their searches.

Replacing random drug tests with impairment or performance tests with probable cause will help restore people's rights and privacy. After all, if someone is not doing their job well or is endangering others, it does not matter whether it is due to drugs, illness, tiredness, depression, anger, or plain incompetence. People are still responsible for their actions and work.

Preventive medical information is available at this Oakland, California needle exchange, to encourage safer behaviors among intravenous drug users. As new needles are given out, old needles are collected and disposed of to prevent any possibility of reuse. Photos by Scott Braley.

Reducing harm: A new model

'Harm Reduction' is an approach to dealing with the 'drug problem' that began in Europe and is attaining international interest and success. Its premise is simple: drugs are here to stay, as they always have been throughout human history, so it seeks to reduce the harm done to the individual user and to society to a reasonable level.

Unlike the zero tolerance or prison/criminal model, harm reduction is a public health model based on inclusivity and helping people rather than on stigmatizing and punishing them. It offers 'treatment on demand' for people having problems with drugs who want to get into recovery. It supports needle exchange programs that provide outreach to addicts, to reduce the sharing of needles and the spread of infectious diseases and to enable people to get into treatment. In some countries methadone is readily available through clinics or local pharmacies. This allows users an effective alternative drug treatment for heroin addiction. It helps them achieve stability and function normally, reducing criminal activity.

In Switzerland, 'heroin maintenance' programs provide safe doses of heroin to addicts in a controlled environment. They have succeeded in improving the health of addicts, enabling them to re-join the workforce and become productive members of society, while reducing the property crimes associated with supporting an expensive and illegal habit.

In the Netherlands, marijuana and hashish are decriminalized as 'soft drugs'. Certain 'coffeeshops' are allowed to sell cannabis to adults, thus providing a safe haven for pot smokers. By this single step, the Dutch have made fewer of their people criminals while drawing taxes from a thriving enterprise. The separation of soft drugs from the criminal underground market also greatly reduces interest in and involvement with 'hard drugs'.

Harm reduction is spreading and gaining increasing acceptance as a workable model. The countries that are incorporating these programs are experiencing lower crime rates and significantly lower rates of drug use than is prevalent in the United States.

Amy Shutkin of the Alameda County Exchange (CA) was arrested for exchanging syringes in May 1994. Photo by Scott Braley.

Bans on needle exchange, limited treatment slots, inconvenient outlets and hours, and overly strict control of methadone access have hampered the effectiveness of such programs in the US. Treatment is a cost-effective alternative to incarceration, costing about $4,000 per year versus $23,000 per year for a prison cell. The implementation of a variety of treatment options and allowing private endeavors to operate harm reduction services would help break the cycle that leads many American addicts back to prison.

Needle exchange programs: A Harm Reduction approach

Epidemic numbers of blood-borne infections have been spread by shared use of hypodermic needles. Despite their illegality, needle exchange programs have been set up throughout the United States in order to slow and track the spread of HIV/AIDS and Hepatitis C among injection drug users.

The concept is simple: replace used syringes with free clean ones and discourage needle sharing to protect the drug users, their sex partners, and their unborn children from the spread of these highly infectious diseases. Drug injection is the primary vector by which these lethal viruses pass into heterosexual society. Studies by the federal Government Accounting Office scientific research arm and the Centers for Disease Control, among others, have come to the same conclusion. In February 1998 federal Secretary of HHS Donna Shalala said, "Needle exchange reduces the spread of HIV/AIDS by up to fifty percent and does not increase drug use." The federal government has again failed to act on scientific reality, so it has fallen to local communities and governments to step in and provide such services and risk prosecution.

In addition to clean syringes, clients are given condoms, alcohol wipes, and in some cases bleach (to kill viruses, when used correctly), and non-judgmental health information about safe sex and drug practices. Most importantly, if less understood, the syringe exchange treats its clients with the respect

Needle exchange support rally in Oakland. When the needle exchange workers were prosecuted, a jury acquitted them. Photo by Scot Braley.

and dignity that each human being deserves. In many instances, these programs are the only way to reach people who need help, and to refer them to drug treatment programs.

Needle exchange programs are common in Europe and have been endorsed by public health organizations, including the World Health Organization, American Medical Association, the National Academy of Science, six federally funded studies, and two former Surgeons General — C. Everett Koop and Joycelyn Elders. A 1996 survey showed that two-thirds of the American public supports needle exchange, too. The US government, however, refuses to fund them.

Federal policy limits treatment slots and thwarts both the development and availability of critical treatment options, such as methadone and ibogaine, that can help get people off hard drugs. Instead, the US relies on a program of forced abstinence by arresting addicts — and those who try to help them.

Offering a second chance

Once someone is caught in the prison system, help is needed to prevent them from returning. Studies show that treatment and counseling in prison along with meaningful job training and education assist inmates in making life changes that benefit them on the outside. Budget cuts that take away these programs facilitate the creation of 'hardened criminals' who will someday get out of prison. Providing opportunities in prison is cost-effective in reducing recidivism.

Prisoners who spend years behind bars need a helping hand upon release to facilitate an easier adjustment back into society. Counseling to deal with their isolation, anger, and readjustment along with job placement to help people find work is a worthwhile investment in reducing recidivism and the ultimate costs of incarceration. The current political trend to eliminate student loans, housing or welfare benefits for released felons is not only an extension of punishment for those who have already served their time, but is a cruel measure with ultimately costly consequences.

At some point they will be released. Offering transitional help to prisoners when they re-enter society will benefit everyone.

Juries serving up justice

Any citizen may eventually be called to serve on a jury in a drug case. If so, it is your duty not merely to judge the facts, but also to act in the interest of justice.

Despite what a judge may say, it is always within your power as a juror to vote your conscience. This fundamental legal principle is known as jury nullification. It has been a judicial tradition since the Magna Carta. In practice, it may require voting to acquit a defendant despite the evidence, if you believe the law is inherently wrong, is unjust in its application, or results in a disproportionate, cruel or unusual punishment.

A juror is not required to explain his or her vote, but may simply state, "In my personal opinion, the prosecutor has not proved beyond a reasonable doubt that this particular defendant is guilty of a crime. I am not convinced, so I vote to acquit and stand by that decision." That's all it takes.

Anything else you say may get you into trouble and not help the defendant, since judges and prosecutors prefer to ignore this right in the courtroom and may withhold this information about your rights as a juror. But, it is your power — and duty — to act as a humane balance on the scales of justice.

Negotiating to end the Drug War

Many of the people in this book and thousands of others like them simply do not belong behind bars at all. No one deserves the kind of human rights violations that are embodied in the Drug War. It's time for human rights to be fully respected.

What you can do to help

There are lots of things you can do to get involved and help effect positive change. Following are some basic suggestions:

1.   Educate yourself and be vocal. Talk to others about what you have learned.
2.   Write letters to editors of newspapers and magazines. Call into talk shows and express your views.
3.   Contact your elected officials at all levels of government. Call or write them and tell them you want them to work for legislation that respects human rights and against unjust laws. Educate them on the issues. Hold them accountable.
4.   Work with local government, schools, community and professional groups and organizations to effect changes in policies and priorities.
5.   Get involved with your school curriculum. Demand honest drug education.
6.   Use your skills. Students can write papers, essays, speeches, and do research on this topic. Writers, musicians, artists, and actors can be especially creative in spreading the message of tolerance and reform through various media. Business owners can enforce a "no drug testing" policy in their businesses. Attorneys can challenge the laws in court and help defend victims of the Drug War, pro-bono.
7.   Use the power of the ballot box to vote for change. Run for office on a reform platform or help sympathetic politicians get elected. Work on voter initiatives or petitions.
8.   Join or donate to a local or national group that supports reforms. Volunteer to help out or organize events that bring attention to these issues.
9.   Become an Internet activist. Do more research, network with people who have the same interests, and blast your opinions to a wide audience. Link your web sites.

Whatever you do, start doing it now, before it's too late.

One of the few good things about a drug policy based on the war model is that it gives us historical models to draw upon of peace talks and negotiated settlements to end the war, as well as the Geneva convention protections of civilians and POWs from torture and abuse. Call a cease fire and release the civilian noncombatants, i.e., non-violent drug offenders. After all, a general amnesty was issued by President Carter to pardon draft resistors and heal the wounds of the Vietnam War.

The Universal Declaration of Human Rights Article 8 states, "Everyone has the right to an effective remedy by the competent national tribunals for acts violating the fundamental rights granted him by the constitution or by law." The First Amendment to the US Constitution promises we can "petition the Government for a redress of grievances."

The question is how do we do that, and to that end, we are calling for a Drug War Truce. This would be a first step towards a reinstatement of full human rights and protections for each individual. We ask you to sign and support the Drug War Truce included in the appendix of this book.

Making a difference

We hope that this book has empowered you with information and made you aware of the urgency of the situation. It's time to take a stand and defend what precious few liberties we have left. It's time to come to the aide of our country and of our countrymen.

There are networking opportunities in the appendices of this book; a truce to sign, human rights to invoke, active groups to contact. We have the power to change the future, and indeed we must. Together we can make a difference; together we can still make America a free country, with liberty and justice for all.

The next step is yours. Make it a good one.

Afterthoughts

When the Drug War comes knocking at your door

I didn't volunteer for the Drug War. It came to me in February 1991 in the form of a warrantless search of my home in San Francisco.

The probable cause? Unknown to me, my companion, Steven, was engaged in a plan to sell drugs. Federal agents in search of evidence came to the house, having prior knowledge that it was an address where he was known to reside. Thus began a long journey through the criminal justice system, and my introduction to America's War on Drugs. Steven's arrest and subsequent incarceration are indelibly marked in my mind. Our lives were forever altered from that day forward ... shattered lives.

Our story is not unlike many of the prisoner stories in this book. We experienced the full impact of government search and destroy missions. Threats of asset forfeiture, the seizure of personal belongings, encounters with zealous prosecutors and DEA agents, judges, courtrooms, jails, and endless legal proceedings. The finale — for Steven, a punishment of five years in federal prison. But it did not stop there. He was also slapped with a hefty criminal fine, random urine testing, and four years of supervised release after prison.

I never condoned Steven's drug dealing, yet the punishment seemed unfair. Outraged, angry and sad, I watched him go off to do his time. The future loomed, uncertain for him, for me, for us. It didn't take long to realize that what was happening to us was much, much bigger than our own personal experience. In December 1991, I found my way to a national organization called FAMM (Families Against Mandatory Minimums). Their goal was to expose and ultimately repeal the cruel and long sentences being meted out to non-violent drug offenders. I quickly became involved with FAMM activities and yes, I volunteered on my own accord to be a coordinator in California. Armed with a local membership list, I began contacting other individuals, including prisoners and family members. What a relief it was to share my experience with others who understood. I was alarmed to learn how many people had been caught up in the same situation — especially, the growing number of women prisoners.

We all know the adage, "Necessity is the mother of invention". Well, the rest is history. I became an activist with a cause, committed to using constructive ways to help myself and others express their rage against the Drug War machine. It was a true call to arms, and I knew it would be a long haul—day after day, year after year.

I've learned many things the last seven years, and the most prominent thought which stands clearly in my mind is this: THE DRUG WAR IS WRONG! There is nothing good about it. It's mean spirited, destructive, negative and greedy. It's downright Un-American. This book provides a very broad picture; some history, some facts, some figures. But most of all, this book is about the human face of the Drug War, as seen and told through real life testimonies.

We hope you are scratching your head and asking yourself—how could these events happen in America; but the stark reality is that all this is true. We are facing a made-in-America debacle that undermines the very principles upon which a democratic society is built.

Where do we go from here? I found the following quote many years ago. Sadly, it is from a man who ultimately lost his battle with AIDS. I find it inspirational and it has given me strength at times when I felt like giving up. I suggest copying it and keeping it with you.

"Commitment is what transforms a promise into a reality. It is the words that speak boldly of your intent. And the actions which speak louder than the words. It is making time where there is none. Coming through time after time, year after year after year. Commitment is the stuff character is made of, the power to change the face of things. It is the daily triumph of integrity over skepticism"

In our introduction, Chris Conrad reminds us, "We are all in this together." Mikki Norris notes in the forward, "Be part of the solution, not part of the problem". I say, "Beware. Silence is the real threat." Commit your voice to end this phony Drug War. Do not wait until the day that you may hear your own words echo, "And then they came for me".

— *Virginia Resner*

Appendices

Call for a Drug War Truce With Peace Negotiations

Preamble: No civilized nation makes war on its own citizens. We, the People, did not declare war on our government, nor do we wish to fight its Drug War. Hence, we now petition for redress of grievances, as follows:

Whereas any just government derives its authority from a respect of the People's rights and powers; and

Whereas the United States government has resorted to unilateral military force in the Drug War without any good faith effort to negotiate a peace settlement;

Therefore, We hereby call for a Drug War Truce during which to engage our communities and governments in peace negotiations, under the following terms:

Article 1: The US shall withdraw from, repudiate, or amend any and all international Treaties or agreements limiting its ability to alter domestic drug policy.

Article 2: No patient shall be prosecuted nor any health care professional penalized for possession or use of any mutually agreed upon medications.

Article 3: Drug policy shall henceforth protect all fundamental rights, as below:

1. Each person retains all their inalienable, Constitutional, and Human Rights, without exception. No drug regulation shall violate these Rights.

2. The benefit of the doubt shall always be given to the accused and to any property or assets at risk. Courts shall allow the accused to present directly to the jury any defense based on these Rights, any explanation of motive, or any mitigating circumstances, such as religion, culture, or necessity.

3. No victim: no crime. The burden of proof and corroboration in all proceedings shall lie with the government. No secret witness nor paid testimony shall be permitted in court, including that of any government agent or informant who stands to materially gain through the disposition of a drug case or forfeited property. No civil asset forfeiture shall be levied against a family home or legitimate means of commercial livelihood.

4. Issues of entrapment, government motive, and official misconduct shall all be heard by the jury in any drug case, civil or criminal. Government agents who violate the law are fully accountable and shall be prosecuted accordingly.

5. Mandatory minimum sentences undermine our system of justice. The jury shall be informed of all penalties attached to any offense before deliberating a verdict. Courts shall have discretion to reduce penalties in the interest of justice.

Article 4: We propose a Drug War Truce and call for the immediate release of all non-violent and, aside from drug charges involving adults only, law-abiding citizens.

Article 5: No non-violent drug charges involving adults only shall be enforced or prosecuted until all parties have agreed to, and implemented, a drug policy based on full respect for fundamental Rights and personal responsibility.

Epilogue: We proclaim, "Give Drug Peace a Chance."

Endorsed by:

Name _____

Address _____

_____

Phone _____

Email _____

For further information or to help advance the Drug War Truce, write to:
Family Council on Drug Awareness PO Box 1716, El Cerrito, CA 94530. USA

UN Universal Declaration of Human Rights

(Adopted in 1948. Excerpts from the preamble and text.)

Whereas recognition of the inherent dignity and of the equal and inalienable rights of all members of the human family is the foundation of the freedom, justice and peace in the world. ...

Whereas it is essential...that human rights should be protected by the rule of law.

Whereas the peoples of the United Nations have in the Charter reaffirmed their faith in fundamental human rights, in the dignity and worth of the human person and in the equal rights of men and women and have determined to promote social progress and better standards of life in larger freedom.

Whereas Member States have pledged themselves to achieve, in cooperation with the United Nations, the promotion of universal respect for and observance of human rights and fundamental freedoms.

Now, therefore The General Assembly proclaims this Universal Declaration of Human Rights as a common standard of achievement for all peoples and all nations, to the end that every individual and every organ of society, keeping this Declaration constantly in mind, shall strive by teaching and education to promote respect for these rights and freedoms and by progressive measures, national and international, to secure their universal and effective recognition and observance....

Article 3. Everyone has the right to life, liberty and the security of person.

Art. 5. No one shall be subjected to torture or to cruel, inhuman or degrading treatment or punishment.

Art. 8. Everyone has the right to an effective remedy by the competent national tribunals for acts violating the fundamental rights granted him by the constitution or by law.

Art. 9. No one shall be subjected to arbitrary arrest, detention or exile.

Art. 10. Everyone is entitled in full equality to a fair and public hearing by an independent and impartial tribunal, in the determination of his rights and obligations and of any criminal charge against him.

Art. 11.1. Everyone charged with a penal offense has the right to be presumed innocent until proved guilty according to the law in a public trial at which he has all guarantees necessary for his defense.

Art. 12. No one shall be subjected to arbitrary interference with his privacy, family, home or correspondence, nor to attacks upon his honour and reputation. Everyone has the right to the protection of the law against such interference or attacks.

Art. 16.3. The family is the natural, fundamental group unit of society and is entitled to protection by society and the state.

Art. 17.2. No one shall be arbitrarily deprived of property.

Art. 18. Everyone has the right to freedom of thought, conscience and religion: This right includes freedom to change his religion or belief, and freedom, either alone or in community with others and in public or private, to manifest his religion or belief in teaching, practice, worship and observance.

Art. 23.1. Everyone has the right to work, to free choice of employment, to just and favorable conditions of work and to protection against unemployment.

Art. 25.1. Everyone has the right to a standard of living adequate for the health and well-being of himself and of his family, including food, clothing, housing, medical care and necessary social services....

Art. 26.1. Everyone has the right to education....

Art. 26.2. Education shall be directed to the full development of the human personality and to the strengthening of respect for humans rights and fundamental freedoms. It shall promote understanding, tolerance and friendship....

Art. 26.3. Parents have a prior right to choose the kind of education that shall be given to their children.

Art. 27.1. Everyone has the right freely to participate in the cultural life of the community, to enjoy the arts and share in scientific advancement and its benefits.

Art. 29.2. In the exercise of his rights and freedoms, everyone shall be subject only to such limitations as are determined by law solely for the purpose of securing due recognition and respect for the rights and freedoms of others and of meeting the just requirements of morality, public order and the general welfare in a democratic society.

Art. 30. Nothing in this Declaration may be interpreted as implying for any State, group or person any right to engage in any activity or to perform any act aimed at the destruction of any of the rights and freedoms set forth herein.

Resources

Human/Civil Rights

American Civil Liberties Union
(ACLU)
125 Broad Street, 17th Floor
New York, NY 10004
Phone: (212) 344-3005
www.aclu.org

American Society for Action on Pain
(ASAP)
P.O. Box 3046
Williamsburg, VA 23187
757- 229-1840
www.actiononpain.org
(Chronic pain advocacy)

Amnesty International
304 Pennsylvania Ave, SE
Washington DC 20003
212- 807- 8400
www.amnesty.org

Civil Liberties Monitoring Project
(CLMP)
PO Box 544
Redway, CA 95560
707-923-2099
www.civilliberties.org
(Northern Calif. focus, CAMP)

Human Rights and the Drug War
Exhibit /Human Rights 95 (HR 95)
PO Box 1716
El Cerrito, CA 94530
510-215-8326
www.hr95.org

Human Rights Watch
485 Fifth Ave.
New York, NY 10017-6104
212-972-8400
www.hrw.org

Crime / Drug Policy/ Research / Information

Center on Juvenile and Criminal
Justice (CJCJ)
1622 Folsom Street, 2nd Floor
San Francisco, CA 94103
415-621-5661
www.cjcj.org

Common Sense for Drug Policy
3619 Tallwood Terrace.
Falls Church, VA 22041
703-354-5694
www.drugsense.org

Criminal Justice Policy Foundation /
National Drug Strategy Network
1899 L Street, NW, Suite 500
Washington DC 20036
202-835-9075
www.cjpf.org, www.ndsn.org

Drug Policy Foundation (DPF)
4455 Connecticut Ave., NW, Suite B-500
Washington DC 20008-2302
202-537-5005
www.dpf.org

Efficacy
P.O. Box 1234
Hartford, CT 06143
860-285-8831
www.efficacy-online.org

Family Council on Drug Awareness
(FCDA)
PO Box 1716
El Cerrito, CA 94530

Justice Policy Institute / Center on
Juvenile and Criminal Justice
2208 Martin Luther King Jr. Ave., SE
Washington DC 20020
301-565-2009
www.cjcj.org

The Lindesmith Center (East)
400 West 59th St.
New York, NY 10017
212-548-0695
www.lindesmith.org

The Lindesmith Center (West)
2233 Lombard St.
San Francisco, CA 94123
415-921-4987
www.lindesmith.org

Mothers Against Misuse and Abuse
(MAMA)
2255 State Rd.
Mosier, OR 97040

541-298-1031
www.mamas.org

Multidisciplinary Association For
Psychedelic Studies (MAPS)
2121 Commonwealth Ave.,
Suite 220-A
Charlotte, NC 28205
707-334-1798
www.maps.org

Partnership for Responsible Drug
Information
14 West 68th St.
New York, NY 10023
212-873-2982
www.prdi.org

RAND (Research institute)
1700 Main Street
P.O. Box 2138
Santa Monica, California 90407-2138
310-393-0411
www.rand.org

The Sentencing Project
918 F Street, NW, Suite 501
Washington DC 20004
202-628-0871
www.sproject.com

Legal Reform Groups

Families Against Mandatory
Minimums (FAMM)
1612 K Street, Suite 1400
Washington DC 20006
202-822-6700
www.famm.org

Forfeiture Endangers American
Rights (FEAR)
PO Box 15421
Washington, D.C. 20003
202-546-4381
www.fear.org

Fully Informed Jury Association
(FIJA)
POB 59
Helmville, MT 59843
406-793-5550
www.fija.org

Harm Reduction/ Needle Exchange

AIDS/HEPATITIS Prevention Action Network Inc. (APAN Inc.) / HCV Global Foundation
1406 Madison Avenue
Redwood City, CA 94061-1550
650-369-0330
email: joey4rigs@aol.com

Harm Reduction Coalition (HRC)
22 West 27th Street, 9th Floor
New York, NY 10001
Tel: (212) 213-6376
www.harmreduction.org

National Association of Methadone Advocates (NAMA)
435 Second Ave.
New York, NY 10010
212-595-NAMA
www.methadone.org

North American Syringe Exchange Network (NASEN)
535 Dock Street, Suite 112
Tacoma, WA 98402
206-272-4857
www.nasen.org

Medical Marijuana / Marijuana / Hemp

Americans for Medical Rights (AMR)
626 Santa Monica Blvd., Suite 41
Santa Monica, CA 90401
(310) 394-2952 f: (310) 451-7494
email: amr@lainet.com
(medical marijuana, only)

Business Alliance for Commerce in Hemp (BACH)
PO Box 1716, El Cerrito CA 94530
510-215-8326. Conradbach@aol.com

Cannabis Action Network (CAN) / Positive Solutions
2560 Bancroft Way # 140
Berkeley, CA. 94704.
510-486-8083
psg@tdl.com

Hemp Industries Association (HIA)
POB 1167, Occidental, CA 95465

707-874-3648
www.thehia.org

Marijuana Policy Project (MPP)
POB 77492, Capitol Hill
Washington DC 20013
202-462-5747
www.mpp.org

National Organizaion for the Reform of Marijuana Laws (NORML)
1001 Connecticut Ave. NW, # 1010
Washington DC 20036
202-483-5500
www.norml.org

On-line Activisim / Information

Drug Reform Coordinating Network (DRC Net)
2000 P St., NW, Suite 615
Washington DC 20036
202 293-8340
 www.drcnet.org,
www.druglibrary.org

Media Awareness Project / DrugSense
POB 651, Porterville, CA 93258
800-266-5759
www.mapinc.org /
www.drugsense.org

Prisoner Advocacy / Prison Issues

American Friends Service Committee
1515 Webster St., Oakland, CA 94612
510-238-8080

Families with a Future (Calif. only)
1301 Henry St., Berkeley CA 94709
510-527-9524
www.igc.org/justice/fwf

JusticeWorks Community
1012 8th Ave., Brooklyn, NY 11215
718-499-6704

Legal Services for Prisoners with Children (Calif. only)
100 McAllister St.
San Francisco, CA 94102
415-255-7036 ext.311

National Lawyers Guild/ Prison Law Project
558 Capp Street
San Francisco, CA 94110
415-285-5067

The November Coalition
795 South Cedar, Colville, WA 99114
(509) 684-1550
www.november.org

Prison Activist Resource Center
POB 339, Berkeley, CA 94701
510-845-8813
www.igc.org/prisons

Government sites

Bureau of Justice Statistics
810 Seventh Street, NW
Washington, DC 20531
www.ojp.usdoj.gov/bjs

Federal Bureau of Prisons (BOP)
320 First Street N.W.
Washington, D.C. 20534.
202-307-3198
www.bop.gov

Drug Enforcement Administration (DEA)
801 I. St., NW
Washington, D.C. 20001
202-305-8500
www.usdoj.gov/dea/

Executive Office of the President Office of National Drug Control Policy (ONDCP)
Washington, D.C. 20503
www.whitehousedrugpolicy.gov

U.S. Sentencing Commission
One Columbus Circle, N.E.
Washington, DC., 20002-8002
www.ussc.gov

POW contacts from this book

If you wish to contact any of the prisoners mentioned in this book, please contact Human Rights and the Drug War, PO Box 1716, El Cerrito CA 94530.

Index

Charts / UDHR

Artwork and Poetry